"Sage advice, delivered in a clear and humorous manner. Even a lawyer has a difficult time debating the merits of this book."

Klymshyn has done it again. He always cuts to the chase with his wit and wisdom. Filled with practical thoughts and ideas, this is a must-read book for every sales professional who wants to rise to the top of their profession.

How to Sell without Being a JERK! is another tool in our kits to help us survive and succeed in today's world, where sometimes you just have to laugh at yourself—or you leave that job to other people. John's writings are as insightful as they are infectious—good humor and good thoughts help make a useful point. His thought-provoking words and real-world examples really tell a worthwhile story. We are all humans in training and occasionally we need a little direction to really grasp the lesson for today.

Klymshyn's high-energy writing, along with his humor, makes this entire book fun and practical. He addresses discipline, dedication, and passion—all of these will help you be a successful (non-JERK) salesperson!

—Merry Ewing
VP of Affiliate Sales
The CW Network

How to Sell without Being a JERK! provides readers with an understanding of how to make professionalism, knowledge, trustworthiness, responsiveness, honesty, and respect for your customer part of a repeatable sales process in your professional sales life. John's latest work outlines the essential elements of selling with integrity and how this approach will ultimately lead to increased success and professional satisfaction.

—Máire O'Dwyer Houston
Strategic Account Director
Global Sales
Yahoo!

John has dedicated his entire career to examining and teaching the critical characteristics (or in his words, painful selling truths), of very successful salespeople. This book summarizes and highlights these findings. It is a must read for first-time salespeople, and it is a book that should be reread once-a-year by every salesperson who takes their career to heart!

—Bob Dean
Executive Vice President-Managing Director
Grubb & Ellis, Sacramento California

How to Sell without Being a JERK!

How to Sell without Being a JERK!

The Foolproof Approach to the World's Second Oldest Profession

John Klymshyn

WILEY

John Wiley & Sons, Inc.

Published by John Wiley & Sons, Inc., Hoboken, New Jersey.
Published simultaneously in Canada.

For general information on our other products and services or for technical support, please contact our Customer Care Department within the United States at (800) 762-2974, outside the United States at (317) 572-3993 or fax (317) 572-4002.

Wiley also publishes its books in a variety of electronic formats. Some content that appears in print may not be available in electronic formats. For more information about Wiley products, visit our web site at www.wiley.com.

Library of Congress Cataloging-in-Publication Data:

Klymshyn, John.
  How to sell without being a jerk! : the foolproof approach to the world's second oldest profession / John Klymshyn.
      p.   cm.
    Includes bibliographical references and index.
    ISBN 978-0-470-22455-7 (cloth)
  1. Selling.   2. Sales management.   I. Title.
    HF5438.25.K598   2008
    658.8'1–dc22

                                                          2007035348

Printed in the United States of America.

10   9   8   7   6   5   4   3   2   1

To Bill "Ronnie" Hobson, the greatest example of strength, faith, and nonnegotiable standards I have ever known.

Contents

Foreword

L et's face it, we all sell. Have any relationships? Ever spin anything to your significant other to put it in its best light? Or simply try to get what you want? You *sell*!

Have a job? Ask others for support for your positions on issues, or your position in the organization? You *really* sell!

Have kids? Believe me—you sell.

If you buy this notion, then why is "sell" a pejorative? I believe it is simply the way people approach the process of getting others to do what they want them to do that has perpetuated this negative connotation—the perception that selling is not a profession. Does that mean if we only sold "softer," it would be all right?

Or is it something deeper that bothers us about selling for a living, as if selling assumes there is no merit in what is being sold?

John Klymshyn's *How to Sell without Being a JERK*! has some answers for all of us with any unease or hang-ups about selling or "being sold."

I've been fortunate to have been introduced to John in the context of his sales training programs. As the COO of a major region for a global real estate sales company, my job includes recruiting the best talent, assessing competencies of onboard sales staff, and providing educational experiences for the new staff to bring them up to speed quickly. From there, we then manage the opportunities to generate revenue. Because we provide a service to companies looking to lease, buy, finance, or sell commercial real estate, we are squarely in the middle of the so-called sales process. In essence, we only get paid for our service if we close deals on behalf of our clients.

So, if we don't "sell," we don't eat.

Many of the principles in the book were developed during John's sales career and refined further as he engaged salespeople from a wide variety of professions in his training exercises. The sessions are extremely helpful in getting people past their own reservations about the selling profession. He gives people practical, useful approaches that actually sell well, if you will pardon the expression. In fact, John has never left the world of active selling, since he does his own marketing of his services to existing and new clients.

The catchy title aside, what distinguishes this book, and John himself, are the commonsense basics that apply to all of life: Tell people the truth, tell them why you are talking to them and what you are seeking to accomplish, and *listen* to what you hear in return. If it matches, *maybe* you will make a sale. If it doesn't, better to know quickly and move on—and do so with grace, style, and humanity.

In the end, selling is far from a negative. When done right, it is one of the helping professions and, indeed, an honorable one.

—Joseph R. Harbert
Chief Operating Officer, New York Metro Region
Cushman & Wakefield

Acknowledgments

It is the driving motivation of my life to share great ideas and hearty laughs, in life and in my writing. I have yet to accomplish anything worthwhile without lots of help and encouragement from an eclectic, funny, and passionate group of people.

I want to thank the following people who influenced or contributed to how I thought about, and accomplished the completion of, this book:

Terri, my wife, for suggesting the title of this little book. Although she wanted something a bit stronger, we agreed that the title we chose made a unique statement.

Sandra Sellani, a colleague, the "goddess of marketing," a wordsmithing genius, and the author of the subtitle of this book.

John Elston, for not letting me get away with accepting anything less than greatness in what I do, how I do it, and how much I enjoy it all.

Shannon Vargo, for her approach to working with authors like myself. She beat me over the head in a gentle, professional way, ensuring that this book (in my opinion) is my best writing ever.

Matt Holt, for being a good storyteller and a great seller, and for the insight and wisdom to make me one of his authors.

Tim Pulte, for encouragement and connections that will last me a lifetime.

Dave Lakhani for asking a great question and opening a very wide door.

Kelly Hackney, for creative juice.

Lauren, my daughter, for debates that make me think.

John III, for showing me how creative geniuses look, act, and think (and for putting me on youtube.com [search: "klymshyn"]).

Friends and colleagues, who shared their "Painfully True Selling Stories."

Every person who responded to *The Ultimate Sales Managers' Guide.* Your feedback has been an inspiration.

Introduction

I'm guessing you've met your share of salespeople you thought were jerks. We all have. Yet, if you are in sales, how could you possibly want someone to think that about you?

If you are just beginning your career in sales, *How to Sell without Being a JERK!: The Foolproof Approach to the World's Second Oldest Profession* is the book for you. Or if you have been in sales for some time and are unwilling to be stereotyped as a "typical salesperson," and, at the same time, have always felt that there was something missing from your sales approach, this is the book for you, too. This book is also for those of you who make buying decisions and deal with salespeople regularly.

Think about these two questions:

- Why are people in sales positions so often maligned?
- Why do so many of us dread being called on by certain salespeople?

We've all had horrific sales experiences. Now, I'm not talking about the kid knocking on your front door early on a Saturday morning selling candy to help teens in trouble or raise money for his or her basketball team. I'm talking about someone walking in off the street to your workplace to sell printer toner, or commercial real estate services. Or that person from your local, friendly temporary staffing firm who stops by, supposedly *not* to "sell," but to drop off some candy as a gesture of friendship. Every one of them tries very hard not to seem like an intrusion, a pest, or a jerk. And, yet, often that's exactly the impression they leave.

You've probably picked up this book because you wanted to find out whether it is possible to sell successfully without being a jerk. My unqualified answer, of course, is a resounding yes! To set the stage for what I will refer to throughout the book as our "conversation," I would like you to think of the structure of a professional, well-managed sales call in architectural terms, because in my mind, selling conversations (and relationships) are likewise "built." They start with a logical, creative design and follow a blueprint to develop a solid, long-lasting structure. This is never accomplished overnight; and rarely is a business-to-business sale made as a result of a single conversation.

Throughout the book, you will come to see the pitfalls and challenges of building the quality selling structure I want you to design for yourself. To that end, I will share with you real, often funny, stories from the selling life. It always helps us to hear the experiences of others as we make our own way.

I also intend to help you tune into your own good instincts, to understand what prospects are really saying when they speak to you. I stress the importance of listening to get you back in the door a third or fifth time, or however many times it takes to "close."

I have built a successful sales career in the past 23 years, and I have taught many people how to sell successfully without being a jerk. My sales management book, *The Ultimate Sales Managers' Guide* (John Wiley and Sons, Inc., 2006), shares a common thread with this one: my passion to teach a well-considered philosophy of selling, one that focuses on honor and respect for the buyer. Believe me, I have encountered more than my fair share of jerks. I have sold to them, and been sold to by them. I have had them work for me, and fortunately have found a way to convince some of them to leave the profession. As a result, I am confident I can offer you tools that will help you to sell, sell well, and lead a prosperous professional life. How does that sound?

Notice, of course, that I just "closed you." If you are still reading this, it tells me that you are in agreement with me at some level. Since I define "closing" as "coming to agreement," we have already established common ground.

Throughout this book, I am going to discuss typical sales ideas, scenarios, and beliefs. Then I am going to shatter those outdated and self-defeating approaches that prospects can smell a mile away. You know what I mean—the statements or tactics that make prospects think, "This salesperson is a *jerk!*" You'll learn powerful ideas, which not only are fun to try but that have made a lot of people *a lot of money*. And I'll do it using plain, American business language, not fancy-schmancy Ivy League lingo. This, I promise you, won't be a retread of ideas you've read elsewhere. It is a clear-eyed view of what selling all too often is and, more importantly, what it can be when handled properly—that is, a great, fun, exciting, lucrative, and respectable profession.

I have put my heart, mind, body, and soul into defining a sales approach that has taken people to new levels of success. One of the best compliments I ever received came from a client, Sandra Sellani, who over time became a friend and confidant. She told me that what she found unique about my approach to sales, and sales training, was that I had put the humanity back into sales. High praise!

Now it's time for you and I to begin to connect, to begin our conversation. Whether you bought this book or someone bought it for you, I look forward to talking with you. I believe I have something truly unique to share with you about how to sell. Realizing that was like having an epiphany. I hope you have many as you read this book.

If you're tired of cute comments and refried attitude adjustment theories, and of scripted selling approaches that do not allow for the surprising and fun aspects of sales conversations, read on. If you're frustrated by not understanding why you don't sell more, read on! If you've felt that there must be a better way, a more honorable, human approach to sales that will allow you to make more money *and* feel good about what you do, read on. If you want never to sell like a jerk, my smart and alert reader, then read on.

What's So Funny about Sales?

I asked several friends, clients, and colleagues this question as I prepared the original outline for *How to Sell without Being a JERK!*, and I received a variety of answers. Many turned out to be some of the funniest first-person accounts of mistakes, malaprops, goofs, and misstatements I had ever heard. Then, while I was on the phone listening to someone recount his story, through my laughter, I said: "Oh, no! That's painful!" "Painfully *true*," was his immediate response.

This gave me an idea. As in life, there are so many painful lessons to be learned in sales, I thought, why not teach these lessons more effectively by doing what society has done for centuries: tell a story.

That is why, in this book, I have assembled for your reading pleasure and learning enjoyment, eight Painfully True Selling Stories that are both instructive and humorous.

I wonder if anything like what you will read here has ever happened to you?

CHAPTER ONE

WHAT EXACTLY IS WRONG WITH SALESPEOPLE?

B efore we can instruct, correct, heal, and discharge the patient, we must diagnose the problem. The problem I take on in this book is that some (not ALL) salespeople sell like jerks!

Do they act that way on purpose? Is their behavior constant, unending, and unavoidable? Does selling automatically make someone a jerk?

I do not think so.

I have come to the conclusion that I regard selling, and hear the conversations around selling, a bit differently than most people, for a couple of reasons. First, I am proud of the fact that I have been earning a living for 23 years as a salesperson. Second, I have a romantic view of what sales is all about. Sales affords those of us who sell an opportunity to plug into the grand symphony of life. It is the engine of every economy—micro to macro. As Joe Harbert mentioned in his foreword, every time you interact with someone and move that person (or are moved) to a common goal, you are having a sales conversation. So, assuming that is the case, let's do it right! Let's act like professionals, and make sure that when we sell, we are not selling like jerks.

WHERE YOU AND I WILL GO TOGETHER

Let's begin with what compelled you to pick up this book. It might have been a recommendation from a friend or colleague. It might have been happenstance. Maybe the cover caught your eye in a bookstore. Whatever the reason, there was something in the title of this book that on some level resonated with you.

Throughout the book, you can expect the following:

- Real-life, sometimes funny, absolutely true stories about the selling life. I call them "painfully true selling stories."

- Short, to-the-point aphorisms I call "Painful Selling Truths™."

- A defense of the profession—not an apology or an explanation, but a passionate presentation of the case *for* the selling profession, along with an explanation of why there would be no industry or commerce without sales.

- Great ideas, techniques, and strategies you can adopt and adapt immediately, that will help you:

- Not be a jerk
- Have more fun selling
- Make more money

If you like to think, listen, solve problems, connect with people, and have a few laughs while earning a living, then a bent toward selling may be more a part of your personality than you realize.

Wanting to be successful in your career does not make you a jerk. Wanting to close more sales does not make you a jerk. Wanting to earn more money this year than last does not make you a jerk. Thinking that you must be rude, curt, short, brusque, pushy, overbearing, combative, or argumentative, or employ any other mildly annoying way of communicating with people is anathema to what we will discuss in this book. Those behaviors are unequivocal traits of people who sell like jerks.

You and I have the opportunity today to turn the perception of selling on its ear, simply by how we choose to respond and react to the world around us. We can sell like human beings, interested in the overall welfare and success of the people we call on, or we can sell like jerks.

Begin by looking at the methods you use to sell through the lens of someone to whom you sell. Share ideas with your colleagues and friends. Use this book as a springboard for a revolution in selling that improves the perceptions of the profession. Let's make a real difference in the lives of the people we work with and for. Let's have people we sell to (even if they decide *not* to buy from us) speak of us in a positive manner after their interactions with us.

WHY YOU SHOULD LISTEN TO ME

I, your humble servant, have sold to professionals and decision makers in just about every city in the United States. I have also sold to (by which I mean, closed deals with) people in Ireland, England, Holland, and Mexico.

I have sat with people in high-level positions at major corporations. In all of my experience, I have yet to see someone make more money than others simply because he or she was a jerk. Conversely, I have yet to see someone go hungry because he or she chose not to be a jerk.

You and I are familiar with the stereotypical salesperson personality. Salespeople who fit this stereotype are so oblivious to how their attitudes and presentations are perceived that it's clear they do not hear what is coming out of their own mouths. They appear to be in their own world. It's kind of humorous, if you think about it. The fact that they offend, insult, or irritate their clients at any level seems to fly under the scope of their own radar.

I have seen and experienced presentations by salespeople (perhaps you have, as well) that make everyone in the room look around as if to say, "Does anyone else hear what this person is saying? Am I the only one who's thinking, 'What a jerk?'" If you have been in a meeting like this (and cringe at the memory), then the ability to sell without being a jerk holds some attraction to you.

I am not going to make many promises to you in this book, but here is one I will make: If you truly want to sell without being a jerk, you are going to find ideas, tips, and techniques in this book that will:

- Change your thinking.

- Impact your actions.

- Invariably change your results.

Maybe you're protesting, "I don't sell like a jerk, but I know people who do." If this is the case, then use the book to become aware of the mistakes other people make every day so you can avoid them.

TWO VIEWS, ONE GOAL

Selling is a thought-based profession, the intricacies of which are ruled by emotion. This may seem contradictory, but stay with me: I will connect the two lines of thought.

Selling is thought-based; buying is feeling-based. This is one of the few professions where the two parties involved in every interaction act on opposing motivations: salespeople are looking to sell more and more expensive items to customers, who are looking to buy more affordable items. This dichotomy introduces a variable into the dynamic that must be addressed for the relationship to be successful. If the people you sell to do not feel comfortable with you, you will not sell them as much as you might.

Unending debates take place in the theater of American commerce regarding whether buyers need to like you as a person in order for them to buy from you.

I subscribe to the following train of thought:

- People buy based on emotion.

- Salespeople must control the conversation, and be persuasive (yet nonthreatening), to successfully fulfill their job responsibility and serve their customers well.

- Wanting to, deciding to, or continuing to be a salesperson does not automatically make you a jerk.

- You can, with thought and reasonable emotional control, sell without being a jerk.

I, like many in my field, have been insulted and have had my feelings hurt by people who, without any sensitivity, insult the sales profession by saying that it is a nonprofession, or that it does not take much intellect to master. Or they deliver the classic "salespeople are jerks" lines: "I could never sell something to someone. I don't want to give people something they don't want."

Those are just opinions, however, which I consider misinformed, and a bit pedantic.

Don't get me wrong: I do acknowledge that there are ruthless, inconsiderate, unnerving personalities operating as salespeople in the world. Of course I do! Why else would I write this book? But acknowledging the existence of something is not the equivalent of endorsing it.

So, the quintessential, revealing, and probing question is, "Why do some people sell like jerks?"

Without acting or sounding as if I am defending anyone, I will say that based on my extensive research (23 years' worth, across 3 countries and 65 cities, addressing more than 25,000 people), I have found incontrovertible evidence that the twofold reason people most often sell like jerks is:

1. They are in the sales profession because they have run out of jobs that would tolerate poor performance (or have difficulty living up to expectations) and they have

landed in a sales position where their employers fig-
ured having *someone* call on prospects was better than
not having *anyone* do it (not exactly the highest standards there).

2. The person selling like a jerk has a chip on his or her
shoulder.

Like any career, sales is not for everyone. It is for people
who, like me, have a deep need to challenge and prove
themselves, over and again, over long periods of time, to
new and unrelenting, and constantly changing audiences.

Think about that and really examine whether it applies
to you: "prove yourself over and again, to unrelenting,
and constantly changing audiences." There is no "arrival"
in sales. We sales lunatics are constantly looking for the
next challenge, the next more complicated deal, the larger
prospect (or "fish") to land.

These characteristics may sound similar to those required
of someone who has aspirations to be a successful actor or
other type of performer, and there certainly is a good deal
of common ground between the two careers. But the most
relevant analogy I can come up with is that a salesperson
who operates without being a jerk—someone who embraces
the ups and downs of the career, thrives in a competitive
environment, and maintains a cordial, professional approach even when dealing with the most difficult of clients—
is most like an architect.

Architects by nature approach thought and application
in similar ways to professional sellers—salespeople who
sell without being a jerk! Both understand the importance

of planning, setting strong foundations, and incorporating creativity into their daily work. The most significant and distinctive similarity, however, is that both salespeople and architects are focused on designing and building something that is made to last.

A LASTING IMPACT

If you are looking for the quick buck, and don't care to develop a relationship, or even sell to the current prospect again, then you are at risk (whether you mean to or not) of selling like a jerk.

When done right—meaning done well, like a professional who cares about the impression he or she makes on people, and the lasting impact he or she has—there is romance involved in the selling process. It is a dance of decisions and motivations. Salespeople are motivated by quotas, bonuses, and accolades. We earn those by bringing in profitable business. Buyers are motivated by myriad factors. The romance I refer to points to the rarity of two people (or two groups) finding each other, fulfilling each other's needs, and enjoying a healthy relationship for an extended period of time.

The decisions made are based largely on emotional issues, ranging from "I want to look good to my boss, so I have to get this deal" to "I need to make bonus this month in order to have a good vacation, so I am going to jack the profit margin *just a little*" to myriad others.

If you think that no one with scruples or ethics would even think about doing any of the above, you would be wrong. I point these out because I want you to believe you can take my honesty to the bank (and if they give you any money for that, call me right away!).

Walk a Mile toward My Quota before You Criticize

The sales profession has some detractors, as we all know and have experienced. There are countless examples in the mainstream media where salespeople are depicted as "snakes," who live to manipulate people out of their hard-earned money. While a recognized stereotype, it is not the majority rule.

I wrote this book to lend a voice to that larger percentage of salespeople I have coached or taught over the years, to give them a forum from which to demonstrate their love for the profession. In addition to the exhortations I include here, I will indict anyone who is currently selling like a jerk. Please cease and desist immediately! Join my friends, colleagues, students, and clients in setting the profession of sales on a high and sturdy pedestal—not to be worshiped or revered, but to be respected and held in high-enough esteem so that sharp, funny, hard-working people are attracted to, and stay in, the profession for a good long time.

Define Your Dreams

Freedom, wealth, income, prosperity: These add up to the dream for me.

I do not refer to this as the American dream, for several reasons, not the least of which is that other groups (media, social commentators) have appointed themselves the arbiters of that state of mind.

Freedom works for me, because I like work but I *love* play. If I want to build a life for myself, I have to do so in small, incremental, consistent, and disciplined steps.

Selling without being a jerk is as much a discipline as being able to play a musical instrument; both require practice, study, patience, as well as a willingness and open-mindedness to be corrected.

Notice that I did not say "taught" at the end of the previous sentence. I chose the word "corrected" because the personalities most often attracted to sales are often gregarious, extroverted, and highly intelligent. (No, that is not a stroke of people's egos.) Selling requires a high ability to function, think, respond, and modify one's reactions. People who are attracted to repetitive tasks, which do not require creativity in the performance and completion of their standardized tasks, will not be comfortable in sales.

Selling without being a jerk means that although the salesperson is under pressure to perform, he or she never makes reaching quota anyone else's problem.

When you sell without being a jerk, reaching one's quota is rarely a problem. It is a measurement tool—a benchmark—and nothing more.

Do It Well, or Don't Do It at All

Bryon Carney is the managing director of a commercial real estate firm in Phoenix Arizona. He is an excellent salesperson, and a stunningly talented manager. He has a great, simple saying: "If you're going to do something, why not be great at it?"

Bryon and I are big believers in personal responsibility for production in sales.

Whether someone sells like a jerk or not, we must face how difficult this work (selling) is. It can test your mettle—your emotional strength. My simple admonition and warning to people who do not love selling is, "If you don't love it, don't do it!"

No one is going to come to your home and force you to go out into the world and cold-call. You almost have to have a need to do it.

I have talked with, counseled, sat with, and listened to many people who explain the unique challenges and distractions they face, all with the hope that these excuse them from measurable accomplishment. After a while, "the dog ate my lead sheet" just does not justify low performance.

If you are not predisposed to searching out and meeting challenges, if you do not like having your level of performance measured and compared to others with whom you work, or you are not accustomed to having to create opportunities for yourself, you would be best advised to pursue an alternative profession.

Have Fun

Whenever most people encounter others having fun, they respond with a smile. When people hear others laughing, they eagerly anticipate being let in on the joke.

It has been scientifically proven that laughter is good for the body, mind, and soul. Selling affords the luxury of these scenarios being a part of every workday.

If this sounds attractive to you, then the selling profession can offer you a lifetime of income, freedom, and laughter—if you sell without being a jerk.

HOW SELLING WORKS

Every sale is based on a variety of factors, from the marketing offered to the salesperson as support material to the salesperson's passion for what he or she is selling to the determination needed to find the right person, at the right company, at the right time for it all to make sense, and to be valuable to the person (suspect, prospect, or client) choosing to buy.

Note

I will refer to three types of people throughout this book: *suspects*, *prospects*, and *clients*. A suspect is anyone who has a phone; a prospect is anyone who has a phone and who meets some of your criteria as someone to sell to; and a client is someone who has caused you to earn income.

All of the phrases and thought processes here can be represented in terms commonly used in the field of architecture. Laying foundation, building solid frames, designing an appearance that is pleasing to others, creating an experience that people will want to visit over and over again: these are the common tasks set before both architects and salespeople.

Over the course of the book I will identify, explain, and demonstrate how important the conversation is to building relationships, and how multiple relationships, when built properly, will provide you with laughs, opportunities to grow, and a very comfortable income. Are you willing to gamble? Do you feel comfortable risking your future on your own determination and sweat?

Don't kid yourself. People (like me and many others referred to or quoted here) like to make money. I personally want to make more money this year than I did last year. As of this writing, I have the most aggressive (yet realistic) financial income goal I have ever worked toward in all of my years of selling.

Money means different things to different people. To me, it means one thing: freedom. When I am free to do as I please, I tend to be more creative, I tend to make more money, and I have more fun.

Now, before you read and reread the phrase "do as I please" and interpret it as an endorsement of a salesperson creating his or her own work schedule and quota, please understand that this freedom can only be achieved and enjoyed by working very hard for a long, long time.

You may have heard the phrase "freedom is not free." This is entirely applicable to the selling life.

The price for freedom is often paid without an audience. However someone amasses wealth is only of import to you and me as a learning opportunity—nothing more that could be labeled productive.

Throughout this book, I'll survey the mental half-acre our conversation will cover by asking you some questions. I do not expect you to pull out a pen or pencil and mark up the book with your answers (if you did, how could you ever resell it on eBay?).

This book is about getting to the point. As they say in Hollywood, "Cut to the chase!" With that in mind, you can expect at the end of several chapters a brief list of questions (usually five) that will help you remember, work out, or apply the ideas discussed in that chapter or section.

I'll start here with the first five questions:

1. Why am I in sales, anyway?

2. What is my driving motivator?

3. Which is more important to me (you must choose one or the other):
   ○ Money
   ○ Doing the right thing

4. How do I want people I sell to, to remember me?

5. Would I want my spouse, children, parent, or best friend to be in the room when I close a deal?

I am not interested in engaging in a moral debate about sales or sales tactics. This book is my opportunity to hurl hope at the stars, to find out whether what I have learned and taught to many other people over the years can be expanded and applied to you, the readers of this book. It is not a manifesto; this book is about *you, and how you can sell professionally without being a jerk*. It proceeds from one assumption and two goals.

- The assumption is that you want to sell without being a jerk.
- The goals are:

○ To laugh about the realities, pitfalls, frustrations, and brain cramps that occur in the selling life.

○ To offer you some reliable, proven, and easy-to-apply techniques for selling now, and for a long time to come.

THE BOUNDARIES

As a salesperson, I am required to be flexible in order to succeed. As a parent, I have a few nonnegotiable standards. One specific example is that I want my children to be productive people of character. This simple phrase has manifested itself in my life as a constant effort; nothing makes parents more proud than hearing from someone else how much their son or daughter is respected by his or her peers.

I am not so naïve to think that either of my children is perfect, or that everyone will like them. Not everyone likes me. I am sure you are holding the book in stunned silence right now! How could anyone *not* like this author, parent, salesperson, entrepreneur, and all-around great guy?

This book is not my own private therapy session; it is the culmination of experience, pain, frustration, wisdom, and great achievements.

If my edict for my son and daughter is that they be productive people of character, then I am overwhelmingly responsible for holding this standard before them, encouraging them when they have erred, and rewarding them when they demonstrate decisions and actions consistent with the edict.

This is how you and I will build a solid selling foundation. This is how you and I will prepare ourselves for handling and dealing with the occasional emotional earth-quake, which comes with the territory.

You and I must, right now, commit to selling without being a jerk.

So, why do people sell like jerks?

As my wife would say when asked why someone has done something irritating, "Who *knows*?"

This book may not be able to answer that question, but it will answer these:

- Can I sell without being a jerk and still make a lot of money?
- Can I have fun and still win regular, reliable, profitable business?
- Does the author have any idea what I go through as a salesperson?
- What will this book give me, that I can walk away with and *use*?

Construction on your half-acre of mental space has been approved. The blueprint for the development and construction of solid relationships has been submitted and approved according to standards and conventions, which we will explore throughout this book.

Let's get to work!

Painfully True Selling Story #1

I was invited to make a presentation to a very big pharmaceutical company at the Ritz Carlton in Laguna Niguel, California, approximately three hours from my house.

I got up and started driving at 8 A.M., large latte in hand. By the time I arrived at the hotel, I didn't care about the presentation, I just needed to find the ladies' room.

After I did, I rushed through the lobby to the designated conference room and delivered my pitch. At the end of it, one of the five meeting planners who were interviewing me asked, "Did you know that the back of your skirt is up around your waist?"

I twisted around and saw my bare butt covered only by thin pantyhose. I realized that all of the Ritz guests (and staff) must have had quite a sight.

I replied, "Now you've seen the best side of me."

The planner then said, "You've got the job; anyone who can handle what you just did can deal with any situation."

—Andrea Michaels
President
Extraordinary Events
Sherman Oaks, California

CHAPTER TWO

RESPECT IS EARNED

E arning respect and earning money are similar, in that everyone loves to have both, yet not everyone is willing to do what is required to earn them. Selling without being a jerk means that you earn both simultaneously.

There is a fine line between selling to people so that they don't feel they are being sold to and the lesson of Painful Selling Truth #1:

As soon as you start to sell, people can tell.

The good news is that if you sell, you are someone who likes a challenge. If you have been selling for any period of time, you have found a way to sell to people and repeat the experience. Everyone, and I mean everyone, can tell when someone else is trying to sell him or her something. Selling without being a jerk acknowledges and revels in that fact—we don't try to hide it!

OK, time for some bad news (you knew it was coming, right?). Drum roll, please ... respect is earned! Now, that may not sound like something worthy of its own chapter in such a timely and cutting-edge book as this one. It just sounds like common sense. Yet too many of us neglect to act like we know that respect is something we have to earn in every interaction. Instead, we act as if we believe the opposite. We expect people to respect us because we are good at what we do, or because we are interesting. Unfortunately, neither of these attributes holds the key to being successful in the selling profession, or even to getting into a prospect's office.

Respect is complex and intangible, and can be yours only if you earn it. In sales, this means suffering the slings and arrows of denial and rejection. In sales, your performance and capacity for the work are measured from a tight, almost microscopic perspective. From a distance, your career may be represented metaphorically by the image of a huge, beautiful, solid building; but the day-in, day-out perspective is more like watching each and every nail and weld be inspected the minute you put them in place.

All professions have metrics and measurements. Salespeople are accustomed to one looming and constant question: "What have you done for me lately?" Yet before you can begin to count any performance as a success, you have to start to receive invitations to future forward-motion steps in conversations.

The state of the economy, the latest marketing brochure, the unavailability of leads are never reasons that justify missing a quota. At any given moment, someone, *somewhere* is thinking about or planning to buy something exactly like or similar to what you sell. It is your job to find them, connect with them, receive an invitation from them to proceed, and successfully close the sale.

Sounds simple, right?

You are the driving force and key determining factor in your success, and in sales, success is constantly measured against, and compared to, others (your past, the top performer in your region, or even the last person to sit at your desk before they hired you).

If you are not making your projected numbers (number of calls in a day, number of proposals submitted, number of face-to-face meetings, or even number of orders taken or deals lost in a week), there is a reason. The reason is always your responsibility. Unlocking success may require looking deep to find where problem behaviors are.

RESIST SPINNING

Making a living in sales is hard. It takes fortitude, determination, a sense of humor, intelligence, problem-solving skills, an ability to improvise, determination, a consistently high energy level, and determination (did I mention determination already?). It also requires an ability to maintain mental focus. It is easy to *spin*, to look at, touch, read, or think about a particular activity, then get distracted by what you see on your right or your left and jump to that issue because it might be a higher priority (or just more fun to do right now), and then get distracted yet again. Before you realize how many prime selling minutes have passed, you have spun around in a nonproductive circle while your competitors are on the phone, or drafting a letter, or even face-to-face with your prospects.

Being good at selling means being organized and mastering the efficient completion of various tasks at the right time.

This profession is not like acting. If you are good at sales, you will make money. Whereas, even if you were the greatest actor in the world, the many variables outside of your control would affect your opportunity to find regular work. Living 25 miles from Hollywood, California, I see people arriving here every day to pursue their dreams. Many of them will never stop working at jobs outside their chosen craft for that very reason. While waiting tables, they may audition during the day, or they may "really want to direct!" We salespeople don't have to cope with as many uncontrollable variables and challenges.

BE WILLING TO FAIL

I'm a seller. If I have a price list, prospect phone numbers, and a working telephone, I can make a living. Selling successfully takes a combination of persistent activity, avoidance of spinning, serendipity, and hubris. These factors allow me to sell anything to anyone at any time.

You, as someone who wants to sell without being a jerk, have just as much of an opportunity to sell as anyone else. As difficult as facing repeated rejections is, going into each meeting or call with a willingness to fail will actually improve your sales technique. That simple fact never bothers those of us who have been in the game for some time. Admonition is not just for the apprentice.

A word of clarification is in order here, however: Willingness to fail is not the same as having a *predisposition* to failure. We cannot succeed unless we have failed. Failure provides painful but valuable lessons that teach us about ourselves, the world, and the role(s) we might play in it. It also reminds us that failing does not make us failures. I have failed at being self-employed, twice. It took my third try to get it right. How could I possibly have come to understand the value and the requirements of success had I not failed?

This realization is what led me to the great parenting, training, and life-lesson power of Painful Selling Truth # 2:

Experience may not be the most patient teacher, but it is the most effective.

A willingness to fail is by no means a common trait. Many people will avoid risks at all costs, with the rationale that, "If I don't risk anything, I won't lose anything." That type of thinking is not flawed, nor does it make you someone who does not deserve success. But it will not serve you well if you are someone who wants to sell without being a jerk.

Here's a fun exercise: Call or talk to four different people in the next day or so, and ask them, "What does the word 'success' mean to you?" You will be fascinated by the variety of answers you receive. Once you have gathered them, define "success" for yourself. If selling without being a jerk falls in line with your definition, then we have a lot more ground to cover together. "If I am willing to take a risk, I might get a reward" is closer to the mind-set I would like you to adopt.

As someone who has failed more than once (in business, in sales, and in managing others), I would not have the level of confidence in my judgments, recommendations, or decisions that I do without having experienced those painful but memorable failures.

This leads me to another key question: What are you willing to sacrifice to get what you want? I decided early in my selling career that I was willing to sacrifice time, effort, pride, but *not* my "productive person of character" edict.

When it comes to maintaining a productive character, I have always found inspiration in quotations—words of wisdom—from folks who have done something I consider motivational or made a great contribution to society. Let me share an appropriate one with you here.

Alex Zanardi is a famous Formula One racecar driver. Mr. Zanardi lost the lower parts of both of his legs and all but one liter of blood in a racing accident in Berlin, Germany, in 2001. On a talk show, he was telling the host what it felt like to go through this experience. The host asked him what his life was like now. Matter-of-factly, Mr. Zanardi uttered these overwhelmingly simple and motivating words:

"You really appreciate a smooth road only if you have gone through a bumpy one before—and mine was pretty bumpy!"

No one is responsible for your level of production. People may show an interest or even be intimately familiar with your percentage of attainment over the course of a selling month, but the work, the hardship, the stress, and the seat all belong to you.

So, buck up! While selling is not for everyone, if you stay in the profession and, as a result of your hard work, can pay your bills, take an afternoon off once in a while, and can remember the last time you took a vacation, then be thankful you have the personality, strength, and vision to stay with it. Endurance is the key.

Someone once said that character is the ability to complete a task long after the original enthusiasm for the idea has passed. This quote applies to people in the selling profession because they want to make money. Great idea! Yet, many (and I a mean *many*) people tend to leave the profession quickly once they learn how truly difficult it is. It tests you on multiple emotional and psychological levels. Sticking to it requires having the right mind-set, having the right approach. It is about your expectations. It is about your fortitude.

Selling without being a jerk means that you do not treat each call as a do-or-die experience. And you do not regard each sale that does not "close" as a lost sale, because you realize you can only lose something you already have, not something you *might* have had.

MECHANICS AND NUANCE

This selling life can be very emotional; but we can manage emotional ups and downs by sticking to our guns (i.e., knowing why we do this for a living, and not wanting to be jerks) and by practicing an approach that is based on skill and technique.

The technique side of selling is about two things:

- Mechanics
- Nuance

Mechanics tell me which specific actions to take. For example, do I commit the next two hours to making outbound calls? Do I go and visit previous clients and see how things are moving along with their orders, deliveries, and use of what I sell?

All of those are mechanical aspects of the selling profession, and engaging in any or all of them in a given week supports my goal of selling without being a jerk.

Then there is the part of selling that requires patience, thought, responsiveness, and emotional control—that is the nuance side of selling.

It is one thing to dial out to leads in a database, to see if anyone wants to buy anything. It is quite another to go through the process I discussed in Chapter One—to engage the prospect (or suspect, or client) in a conversation about his or her business, not *your* product, service or idea. To do this effectively requires putting nuance into play. Nuance is the subtle, musical difference in the type of questions you ask, the intent behind your visit, and how much you can learn rather than how many features you can spew.

My editor and I had a discussion about the last word of the last sentence. I concede that "spew" does not create a beautiful mental image; but neither does the experience of listening to a salesperson yak (ramble, chatter, natter, etc.) on and on about this feature, this fact, this aspect, or that distinguishing detail. Facts do not sell. Features do not sell.

People sell. Relationships develop when you are a good listener. What sells is the ability and willingness to engage people in conversations about the things they are interested in or concerned about, and selling without being a jerk.

I have a simple definition for selling: "Having people feel good about making a positive decision to move the conversation forward with me, today."

I just reread that, and I realize it may not be simple, but it covers the bases and basics. More importantly, it does not contain any reference to closing, deal making, transactions, commissions, or pricing.

It may seem contrary to the thrust of the selling life, but selling is not about making money. It is about the mental challenge and the tangible reward that comes from doing quality work. It is about the contribution you make when your product, service, or idea helps someone else achieve his or goals. It is about service.

BASIC VOCABULARY

My wife and I love to travel, and we have been fortunate enough to visit numerous foreign countries, most of them not English-speaking. Before we could visit those places with a sense of safety and comfort, we had to learn basic words and phrases—"please," "thank you," "How much is this?" and "Do you serve cheeseburgers?" in several languages. We also had to learn simple customs that seemed, well, foreign. We have yet to have a problem. And learning the basics has helped us to connect with the people in all those places.

I tell you this because in this book, I plan to take you to what may seem like foreign territory. It is my goal that you and I connect via a common language—that language may be the language of music, or business, or humor. If any of these interest you, then we can continue together, and enjoy the trip! Let's begin this phase of our trip by defining simple, key words and/or phrases that I will be using throughout the book.

So here are three basic terms and their definitions. I introduced these briefly in Chapter One, but I want to expand on them here.

- *Suspect*: Referring to someone as a suspect in selling is a way to distinguish a specific type or category of lead or person. A suspect is anyone, anywhere, who might have a remote interest in or need for your product, service, or idea.

- *Prospect*: Quite simply, a prospect is a suspect you have qualified. By "qualified" I mean that they meet specific criteria that *you* have identified. That means you have actually spoken with the decision maker, and gathered qualifying data.

- *Client*: This is someone who has caused revenue to come to your company.

These definitions may seem academic, but one of the thorns in my side is that all too often salespeople refer to someone they are courting (a potential future client, aka a PROSPECT) as an *existing* client. (This is commonly done when a salesperson submits an expense report—particularly for entertaining.) I am adamant that we be careful when we start referring to a particular person or company as a client. No one is a client until they spend money.

To qualify your prospects, ask them these questions:

- What criteria do you usually use to select a vendor/representative/advisor?

- What would you need to know about us before you would consider doing business with us?

- How will you evaluate vendors throughout the year?

- What is the best way for you to determine whether what my company offers will be useful to you down the road?

- How can we help you?

Remember, this is a list of questions to deliver to qualify your prospect. Don't fall prey to the urge to assume that because *we* think they need what we have to offer they agree with us. We have to get them to say it.

This brings me to Painful Selling Truth #3:

When I speak, you hear an opinion. When you speak, we both hear the facts.

The goal is to be *invited* to the next step of the conversation. If you're not, get out of the other person's life! This brings me to Painful Selling Truth #4:

The salesperson who knows when to go away, lives to sell another day.

So when I make the statement that respect is earned, it may seem as though I am stating the obvious, (or, in keeping with the theme of the book: Painfully Obvious!) when in fact it is akin to what my father used to refer to as the problem with common sense: "The problem with common sense is, it's not that common."

I appreciate wisdom like this, because you have to think for a moment to decipher its significance; to give your mind time to grasp the concept; and to view the idea through the lens of previous experiences, which leads, ultimately, to understanding.

SIMPLE GESTURES

Describing something as "simple" implies that what follows is something that anyone can master, or that it is something easily done. I say that as an admonition, because the simple gestures described throughout this section may appear to be simple, but if you exclude them (or others like them), you risk being perceived as someone who sells like a jerk.

My goal is to prevent that from happening to you, by introducing the ways selling without being a jerk can help you earn repeat business and help you to better understand how people think and make decisions overall.

Tom Peters, author of several books on business excellence, is quoted as saying, "People like doing business with people they like doing business with. And they tend to like doing business with people they like."

You may not become best friends with the people you sell to. I think it is wise to be "friendly but not familiar."

Familiarity does not breed contempt; it breeds greater comfort. If someone who buys from you becomes too comfortable with you, he or she will tend to be less shy about asking for concessions and extras when it is time to negotiate. Remember: Clients are in business to make money or save money for their employer. As are you. Don't tip your hand by talking openly with people who buy from you about things like profit margins, costs of sales or acquisitions for your company, or any other secure data that can give your client (or one of his or her competitors) an undue or un-earned upper hand in negotiations. All relationships (especially selling relationships) have an arc that builds, plateaus, and could at some point be in danger of declining. No relationships stay the same. They are all in flux, development, or decline. Don't take this as a knock against having fun with clients. It is essential to do business with people you can have a few laughs with. Just be careful that they are not getting the upper hand.

With that in mind, think about where your relationships with your buyers might go if you get too chummy with them. Every relationship needs to be managed. My definition of the verb "to manage" is, "to get the most out of." This is not to say that you should not have a few laughs with a client. What I am saying is that it's important—vital—to set boundaries and standards, so that when you have to announce there will be an across-the-board fee or rate hike next year, your clients do not use the "But not for *us*, right?" tactic.

I first formulated the definition of the verb "to manage" in my book, *The Ultimate Sales Managers' Guide* (John Wiley & Sons, Inc., 2006). My goal in that book was to set a standard for managing salespeople. In it, I talked extensively about the "impossible profession" (sales management), yet expressed optimism that there are people in the world who could achieve greatness in that profession, become "ultimate sales managers," by practicing and implementing 52 attributes ("simple gestures"). My point here is, the people who run down that road have something in common with you. As a reader of this book, you (at the very least) have a curiosity about how to sell in a way that you will be comfortable with, that will help you earn a significant income, and that you can be proud of.

Simple gestures are those that send a message beyond words. Words may be our stock in trade, but remember: *What you do speaks so loudly I cannot hear what you say.*

The magic behind the gestures listed in this section centers around simple interactions and a consistent message.

A Consistent Message

Your particular mood on any given day is not the concern or the problem of your prospects. That may seem to be a harsh statement, but salespeople who are not completely engaged in what they are doing when they begin their selling day will have less of a chance of closing a sale. By allowing whatever happened at home last night or during the commute to work in the morning to seep into their demeanor and attitude during the selling day, a salesperson is compromising his or her success.

I hold the selling day as a sacrosanct, impenetrable experience. Selling without being a jerk requires that I give the best I have to offer, 100 percent of the time.

You may think that sounds competitive. It is, absolutely. Sales is a competitive game, pure and simple. Every moment that you are not working to engage and involve people in qualifying conversations, and thinking about ways to Move the Conversation Forward™, someone else is.

Hold it! Does that mean someone with an inferior product, service, or idea (I'll refer to this from now on as an *offer*), or even a much less sparkling personality than mine, may be beating me, right now? Even though I fully intend to pick up the phone or knock on that door *soon*?

Regardless of what you or your marketing materials say about your offer, the quality and uniqueness of it are lost if someone from a competitor gets his or her offer in front of the suspect or prospect before you do.

Time is money, as you well know, and every moment you allow to pass during *prime selling time* is a moment lost. Irretrievable. Gone forever!

Have I made my point?

Let's talk for a moment about prime selling time. I am often asked, "What is the best time of day to cold-call?" Or "When should I be doing my follow-up dials?" My consistent answer for over 18 years has been: *right now*.

Do not, dear reader, succumb to belief in the office myth that "You should not call people at *X* hour, because. . . " It is all bunk. Bull. Nonsense. The best time to pick up the phone or walk into a prospect's building is any time between 30 minutes before your typical workday begins and 30 minutes after every other salesperson in your office tells you it's too late. Salespeople (in your office, at your company, and, of course, at your competitors) are going to want you off the field of play. Don't let them keep you out of the game by getting you to buy into the "good times to call" myth.

Every precious second of the selling day must be revered and invested for the greatest possible return. There are many techniques you can use to ensure you invest your time well. For one, The 20 Call Burst™ (described in detail in Chapter Nine) provides a detailed, specific, activity-based approach to making the most of the time you spend making outbound calls. By definition, an outbound call is "any and all calls you make to people with the goal of moving the conversation forward." Hence, this is not limited to cold calls; it includes every single time you reach out to humans with the goal of selling without being a jerk.

Note that I said "making the most of" time. I am not a subscriber to the concept of time management. I do not believe we are powerful enough to manage time. Time marches on all by itself. The issue for me may appear to be semantic (and I can live with that), for it is the language we use that creates the images in our head, which in turn influences our actions and responses in the world.

Cosmic Momentum

Is selling without being a jerk a cosmic activity? *Like, totally, dude. Without question!* Now that I have your attention (and have hopefully made you smile), I believe we all have an impact on the world around us, **and** that that impact goes far beyond the physical. Think about it: Have you ever been humming a song and seen someone recognize the melody and smile? Have you ever said a kind word or phrase to someone and been surprised by his or her appreciation and warm response? If so, then you're aware that the thoughts marinating in our cranium all day have a definite impact on those around us.

Your thoughts impact your actions; your tone of voice invites people into your mind and mood. Thus, the content of each call or conversation must be relegated to the confines of that conversation or call. If the last person you spoke to was rude, and I am the next person on your call list, keep in mind that exchange is neither my fault nor my problem. If you have a "bad call" and then call me with the experience still fresh in your mind, you very well may (even if unintentionally) take some of your frustration out on me. And that is, simply, unfair.

By "cosmic momentum," I mean that the investment of time, effort, and attitude we make generates a force that is hard to touch or see. It can only be felt. When I make a round of calls in the morning, and repeat that activity the following day, and the day after that, things start to get stirred up. I am putting my name out into the cosmos. I am letting people (the universe) know that I am serious, and that I am communicating a consistent message, which is: I live to serve.

I want everyone who hears me speak at a meeting, or who reads this book (or any of my books), to be better at what they do as a result. I want there to be fewer jerks out there selling. I want to lead the charge with this book, to have the jerks replaced by more people with a great sense of humor and a love for the profession.

Similarly, when my desk is devoid of activity, that will be reflected in my sales projections. There is a specific and tangible correlation between activity and momentum. One cannot occur without the other.

So I return to the concept of consistency of message. Every time you "touch" (call, meet with, speak to, or leave a voice mail message for) a suspect, prospect, or client, you are engaging in an activity that is a combination of public relations, sales, marketing, and branding. Each thought and gesture is captured in the mind of the person to whom you are directing your attention.

Consistency of message is impossible to deliver if you are driven by mood, if you let that last call or meeting carry over into the next one. Consistency of message means that every time you call a prospect, he or she hears you deliver your offer—that's all; not your mood or your concern that you did not make quota last month.

Your Sense of *Human*

Selling without being a jerk means that you have to maintain your sense of human. You may have been predisposed to think I would say "sense of HUMOR," but I prefer sense of human. They are so closely related, and need each other in order to survive! I use human both as a personal reminder, and as a verbal attention-getter.

We (all humans) are all frail, fractured, and faulty at some level. But we don't have to take ourselves so seriously that we disconnect from the humor that occurs unexpectedly throughout the day. I have yet to come across a person who heads to work with the thought or goal of making someone else's day miserable. We are all just trying to make it through the workday with some semblance of sanity and shared humanity. A laugh or two makes the day go easier—even worthwhile!

For example, when I make a verbal error while cold-calling (I have forgotten my own name, my company name, and—my personal favorite—who I was calling and why), I admit it to the person. I say, "You know what? I completely forgot who I was calling. Can you help me?"

Yes, this is a risky tactic, but isn't leaving the house in the morning risky? Why not have some fun? Be willing to show you are human! You will find that you connect with a lot more people, especially those who know how to laugh at themselves. Our prospects can be a part of the fun and flow of a great workday.

Or, we can ruin theirs if all we do is try to get them to accept a proposal from us, or go through a Web demo with us, or confirm one more appointment so we can go home for the day. These are not what I consider nonjerk motivations. And, truly, is behaving like this a way to become a productive person of character?

See Beyond Selling

I have always been a fan of taking a unique spin on sales. I have been blessed to make a living teaching top-performing sales professionals how to have more fun and make more money, and I have worked with a lot of people new to the profession who wanted to sell without being a jerk.

When I worked for the *Pennysaver* in Thousand Oaks, California, I introduced to the sales staff reporting to me a concept I called, "seeing through people's businesses." By this I meant they needed to look beyond selling an ad to a business and netting a commission. It meant I wanted them to feel personally responsible for each ad they sold, created, and earned commissions from. I wanted them to believe that each ad they sold would *work*.

In the direct-response advertising world, the title says it all. If the ad does not get the desired response, the ad does not work; and that means the ad will not run for long. Here's the food chain: The ad doesn't work → the customer pulls the ad → the salesperson does not earn commission. To the salespeople, this meant they had "lost" a commission. To that I would say (as I have already here, to you): "You can only lose something you already have."

This may not have made them feel much better, but it did resonate with a few of them; they learned how important is was to not only get the appointment but to create an ad that would work, and to keep the customer engaged long and well enough to complete the committed run. That is when the salesperson could enjoy his or her commission—after it had been earned, and paid.

This is also when I started teaching and preaching Painful Selling Truth #5:

The appropriate time to celebrate the sale is after the commission check clears your bank.

At the *Pennysaver*, we encouraged multiweek commitments from our customers, so that their ads would work for them. I wanted their cash registers to ring, and that image is what I wanted the salespeople to see when they sold a program.

On sales calls, we were responsible for answering the prospect's key questions. We had to see *through* the prospective customers business, to see the desired event of someone walking into the establishment with the ad from the *Pennysaver* in his or her hot little hands. This was verification that the customer had been prompted to visit that business by reading the ad. This also showed that we had reader loyalty and, most importantly, that the ads businesses placed with us translated to a ringing cash register.

By seeing through their prospects' businesses, "my" salespeople (mine in the sense that this five-person team reported to me, and their productivity was my responsibility) started to look at what each business did, as opposed to the type of ad every other business like their prospects had already bought.

By seeing through their prospects' businesses, my salespeople started asking questions that got their prospects talking in detail about who they wanted as customers, where they thought people would travel from to buy from them, and what their ideal customer looked like.

This process proved Painful Selling Truth #6:

The more I listen to what you say the more fascinating you find me.

Effectively, and with much less stress, the connection was made between the salesperson's desire to earn money, the current state of the prospect's business, and how the *Pennysaver* might get them to a future desired state.

The most successful of these five salespeople developed questions that were relevant to their prospects, whose responses indicated how the *Pennysaver* worked. And as a wonderful, ultimate result, registers in small retailers all over the Conejo Valley rang. What a great feeling!

The power of the direct mail, direct response invention called the *Pennysaver* lay in getting into every residential mailbox in every zip code, thereby providing us with significant demographical data. We knew, for example, average income; education level; and number of times people living in any zip code would buy coffee, go to a movie, or buy books about cosmic momentum, sales, or wine varietals. This meant that if business owners could identify their desired customers with any degree of accuracy, we could guarantee that their message would be seen by a large segment of the population that had those characteristics.

On the face of it, this made advertising with us seem to make sense. The challenge from there was determining the type of ad that would generate the response—as opposed to feed the ego of the writer of the copy.

A Really Painful Personal Story

When I first started in the position as sales manager at the *Pennysaver*, I was convinced I had a knack for writing ad copy. (How hard could it be?) One of my salespeople brought in a multiweek program for a mortgage and home equity lender. I told her that I had been struck with the hammer of creative insight, and that she should propose the following headline for the ad: "Who wants money?!"

My thought at the time was that since this company, in essence, sold money, taking this question approach would engage the reader. We convinced the mortgage company to use the tag line, as well as to use it as a predominant headline.

After four weeks, the lender pulled out of its committed run. Why? The ad did not generate a single response. The phone at the lender did not ring, not even once.

I loved the ad. The salesperson loved the ad. Even the client liked the ad. The only person who did not like the ad was the potential customer, the person we had decided would be the best target for the ad, and the accompanying offer.

Show Appreciation

As a life-long musician, I use what I know about music in all my communications. I love the sense of timing required to perform a piece of music, and I love the dichotomy of the structure of a song or composition (time signature, key, tempo) and the fact that all of those are open to interpretation.

Phrasing is both a linguistic term as well as a musical one. Phrasing is when you take an accepted or established form (a musical passage) and express it in a unique way. Your phrasing becomes identified with you, and it helps you to identify with the other musicians in the ensemble and with the people for whom you are playing.

I believe that there are two things that transcend all differences or disconnection among us. One is food (everybody eats, and they all have an opinion about what is good!) and music (just about everybody listens to it and knows what they like and don't like). We may not all agree on what is good, but whatever music we like, we tend to be passionate about it. Our preferences are determined at any given time by our circumstance and mood.

In the same way that music resonates, so do simple gestures designed to show appreciation or gratitude. Nothing goes farther in solidifying long-term buying relationships. It is said that the best reward for a job well done is the invitation to perform more work.

As a salesperson, your objective is to get to the next step of the conversation, on an incremental forward-motion path to a long-term buying relationship.

My friends in the hotel and conference center management industry understand this very well. Rebooking is a beautiful thing to someone who sells hotel meeting space, sleeping rooms, and executive meeting space. This is achieved through long-term, incremental forward steps.

Hotel salespeople and I have something in common. We both consistently sell the same inventory: days on the calendar. As a speaker and trainer, every day on the calendar that goes by that I don't have a presentation, seminar, or speech scheduled translates into lost revenue. Every day that goes by in a hotel where a room is empty translates to lost revenue. Rooms are only profitable if and when they are occupied.

The small gestures of appreciation I make ensure that I continue to book dates in the future. Small gestures add up to long-lasting relationships. Here is a short list of some of the most useful and fruitful small gestures I have both delivered and received:

- Thank your customers for buying from you. This can range from giving gifts (appropriate to the person and situation) to the simple (not easy, but simple) act of simply saying thank you. It requires a bit of humility to say this, but this profession is about risk. If you aren't comfortable saying thank you, this might not be the best profession for you.

- Send your customers a funny advertisement that is relevant to what they do, or what they like.

- Send your customers articles that might be of interest to them from the *Wall Street Journal*, *Time* magazine, or any publication.

- Ask their advice about selling within their industry. They may not give you a list of names to call, but they may give you greater insight into the minds of the people in that particular industry, area, or specialty.

Selling without being a jerk means to feel, think, act, and regularly evaluate the results of your actions.

Let's continue down this exciting (and fun!) path in Chapter Three.

Painfully True Selling Story #2

I was meeting with a VP of *Forbes* magazine. I had taught my account executives, over and over, a simple sales process: ask, listen, respond—in that order.

That's what I *taught*. Here's what I *did*: I jumped right in and said: "One of the reasons you can feel comfortable doing business with us is that we have partnerships with 80 percent of the Fortune 500 companies."

That's right! I used *"Fortune,"* *Forbes'* main competition, as a value proposition. It brought the call to an interesting level, and diverted our presentation.

The silence in the room was deafening.

What I *taught* was to have five silver bullets, or an "elevator speech," prepared, with key value proposition items that differentiated our product, or highlighted a reason to do business with us. What I said to that *Forbes* VP was a great value proposition in general; however, it wasn't right for *that* customer. He was offended because I used his main competition as an example. This might have worked with any other customer, but I wasn't thinking about who I was speaking to.

We were able to turn it around eventually, but I learned a valuable lesson that day: "Be careful about being too robotic; treat every customer differently, and think about *their* agenda not *yours*.

—Dennis Napoliello
VP of Sales
Equinox Fitness

CHAPTER THREE

FOOLPROOF APPROACHES TO THE WORLD'S *SECOND* OLDEST PROFESSION

TAKE A DIFFERENT PERSPECTIVE

One of the most challenging tasks is to accurately examine one's own behaviors. Nevertheless, it is an essential one when the goal is to improve the way we act or react. An effective way to gain a clear perspective on one's own behaviors is to attempt to look at ourselves through the eyes of others.

If you have the opportunity to observe selling habits, styles, and nuances of people who sell, either because you manage salespeople or because you are often on the receiving end of sales pitches, you can use what you observe in these interactions to improve your own selling style. By observing others selling, and being conscious of your reaction to the words they choose and the behaviors they employ, you can better measure how your own words and behaviors are perceived by others.

I have done business with companies that own and manage various "flagged" hotels around the United States. These companies are in business with the major brands (Marriott, Fairmont, Hyatt, Hilton, etc.), and they maintain a certain look, standard, and feel within individual properties, in order to maintain the "flag."

One common practice among these companies to ensure adherence to the "flag" is to hire secret shoppers. Secret shoppers in the hotel field are hired to purchase, consume, rate, and critique the conditions and delivery of a typical hotel room night, meal, and any and all other services offered in the hotels they "shop."

This has always been a dream job of mine. Think about it: You go and stay in a hotel, with all of your expenses covered; you are instructed to expect the highest quality of food, service, and amenities, and determine whether that's what you received. And if that were not enough, you are *paid* for this work!

The "job" side of secret shopping is that you must deliver a detailed report, and you must be able to keep your role a secret (you are bounced out of the program if you reveal why you are at the hotel).

Overall, it must be fun to take notes on every interaction, every meal, and every detail; and it's vital for the hotel to collect this information on its staff, practices, and policies, and find out how they are perceived by customers.

The reason I bring up secret shopping is that I would like to do some with you here, as a way of looking at the selling profession (the world's second oldest!) from the perspective of the buyer.

In the first two chapters I discussed the buyer's mind-set and pointed out how emotional many buying decisions can be. When we look at things through the eyes of the buyer, we can open our minds to new, possibly more direct, avenues to show us where we are and lead us to where we would like to be.

HOW TO SPOT A JERK

One of the best ways to ensure your own understanding of something is to be asked to explain it to someone else. This is the approach I took to writing this book. I never wanted to be perceived as a jerk while I was selling, so I thought about all of the horror stories I had been told throughout the years about what people who *are* perceived this way have done to perpetuate the idea. If you have to explain to someone else how *not* to be a jerk, a great way to do so is to explain what qualifies someone as a jerk.

There are several ways to spot a jerk.

- They sell via fear.
- They are hard closers.

- They call, and call, and call again—without invitation, and after the prospect has tried to let them down easy.

- They apply pressure.

- They are rude to people in your organization.

- They take credit for anything good about the product, service, or idea that they represent.

- They never admit to their own errors.

Let's examine each of these briefly.

Selling via Fear

Selling via fear is a personal choice the salesperson makes. Salespeople who sell via fear are intentionally trying to get their prospects to feel a sense of loss if they do not buy from them. Fear is a powerful motivator, but as a selling method it focuses more on manipulating emotions than on selling customers something they want, need, or could use. (Note: Need is rarely the only reason someone will buy from you.)

Think about that: If my intent is to get you to buy from me because you may lose out in some way if you don't, then I am telling you that *I* am more qualified to determine what is good for you and your company than you are. Do you want someone telling you how to make better decisions? Do you want someone to tell you why your past decisions were uninformed, or worse, plain wrong?

I answer no to both of those questions, and if you do, too, then selling via fear is something you want to avoid.

Believe me, I understand the logic of selling via fear, but I don't endorse it, by any means. The truth is that selling via fear is, at some level, an act of desperation. Sellers who resort to this approach must feel so devoid of options, insight, or sensitivity that they are looking for any method to get customers to buy from them. Desperation is not pretty to witness, nor is it a pleasant emotion to endure.

I can say that from personal experience. As I told you in the previous chapter, I have experienced profound failure in my life. And by profound failure, I mean the typical "pride goeth before the fall" kind of failure. As I mentioned in Chapter Two, I was self-employed two other times before my current incarnation. As of the publication of this book, I will have celebrated nine years in a row of being able to determine my own calendar, pay my bills, and vacation where I choose.

This is a beautiful thing, but when I failed last time (13 years ago) I *really failed*.

In the past, I had been so arrogant I thought that because I believed what I had to offer was of value, many other people would agree. I overlooked the basics of the very simple concept of cash flow when running a small, struggling business. As a result, I lost more money than I made—a *lot* more money than I made. I lost so much because of my arrogance that it cost my wife and me our home.

There have also been times in my adult life when I was not sure what my family's financial situation would be in the next 30 to 60 days. These were tough learning experiences. Experience may not be the most patient teacher, but it's the most effective.

Looking back, I am not sure whether I acted out of desperation as much as I did out of simple need to make a buck; but bouncing emotionally back and forth over that fine line between inspired positive thinking and not knowing what to do next is a difficult spot to be in.

So, bottom line: Selling via fear can be understood, but I will not endorse it. Just because it works does not mean it's right. Selling via fear is demonstrated in unpleasant ways, and it invokes an emotional response in the customer that causes the worst buyer's remorse I have ever seen.

Being a Hard Closer

I have many friends in the selling profession. I have also trained countless people and managed several dozen over my career. So I have seen my share of unique selling techniques and approaches. There are several schools of thought about how important *closing* is. Regardless of the philosophy you subscribe to, it is essential that you close a sale in a professional and considerate manner.

Telling someone "this is your last chance" is a hard close. I have yet to see this technique foster relationship building; conversely, I have seen it result in an immediate order but fail to produce future business. Once you close someone hard, they tend not to want to hear from, talk to, see, or much less buy from you ever again.

Hard closers invariably talk and don't listen. Hard closers are convinced they are right, regardless of the long-term effects or aftershocks of a specific sale or deal.

Hard closing is like twisting someone's arm; it's a great technique for a bully or a hit man, but not for the professional seller. Anyone who closes hard, according to my definition, is a jerk.

Calling Repeatedly

Statistics are used by many to validate their points or positions. I often quote the statistic that 80 percent of all statistics are fabricated. Nevertheless, I am convinced that the following statistics are solid and reliable, because I have counted them, tested them, and verified them personally:

- It takes about three to five outbound dials to a particular account to make contact with a decision maker.

- It takes five to seven conversations with that decision maker to determine whether he or she is qualified. (Recall from Chapter Two that "qualify" means to meet specific criteria.)

This means that you must prepare for multiple "touches" with any given prospect before it is realistic to do business with them. (As opposed to giving them the business, or their experiencing the business end of a stick, or the fact that there is no business like show business.)

Now back to the matter at hand: calling repeatedly. You may think there is a contradiction in my admonition and instruction of the previous two paragraphs, so allow me to explain. When I quote those stats, I am talking about using a measured, specific, and professional approach. I tell people that they should make one call short, or ask one question short, of being annoying.

The logical follow-up question from people who want to learn how to sell without being a jerk is: "How do you know when that is?"

My answer: Once you have gone over the line a few times, you will begin to sense it. You will develop an instinct for it.

There are no shortcuts. One of the most reliable personal learning techniques for me has been trial and multiple error.

Mistakes? I have made a few, and now it's time to face. . . what I have learned:

- Touches must make sense.

- Logical, planned, and disciplined calls and other types of touches to a prospect are part of the selling life.

- Calling over and over again, trying to think of one more reason someone should buy from you, is a close relative to desperation—it is obsession.

- Salespeople do not have to (nor will they, realistically) close every account they call on.

- Not being a jerk requires being sensitive to several possibilities. For starters, the person you are calling on, however qualified you think he or she is, no matter how closely on paper (or the Internet, or a paid-for lead list) he or she seems to meet your qualifying criteria, that person may not feel he or she needs what you have to offer. This does not make the prospect uninformed and in need of educating, especially if you are the one who feels compelled to provide that education.

- The reasons people have for not buying from you are numerous and myriad, from "I don't really think I need that" to the fact that some people are just not going to like you. I know that is hard to believe, so I will repeat it: Some people are just not going to like you. Shocking information for both you and I, but there it is. Accept it and move on.

Let me tell you a true—not painful—story to illustrate these important points.

About 14 years ago, I was fortunate enough to teach a sales course as part of the UCLA Extension offering in Los Angeles. During a break, I was approached by one of the students, who asked if I might be able to work with the sales team at his diamond distribution company in downtown LA.

I jumped at the chance, and during a conversation about Painful Selling Truth #4—*The salesperson who knows when to go away, lives to sell another day*—one of the salespeople attending the course became agitated, because he wanted me to tell him how to get a particular retail storeowner to buy from him.

"I *know* he buys from my competitors! He has to buy from me!" he cried.

I responded: "Don't tell me why you want him to buy from you; explain to me why that person *has* to buy from you."

He couldn't come up with a reason that satisfied anyone, including himself.

Moral of the story: When it is clear someone is not going to buy from you, leave him or her alone!

The logical follow-up question is: How do you know when someone is not going to buy from you?

Gut Instinct

Success in any endeavor you pursue requires a combination of trial and error, unconscious learning, and a little bit of gut instinct. Gut instinct is developed over time. If gut instinct were transferable from one person to another, it would be wonderful and dangerous at the same time. It would be wonderful because more than one person would be able to benefit from another individual's experience; it would be dangerous because people would have access to knowledge without having to earn it. They would rarely value it or treat its acquisition with much respect. Gut instinct is reliable, powerful, and useful because as you develop it, you begin to trust it more.

Imagine if you could fast-forward your life at will. (There was a sci-fi film made about a similar concept. Science fiction has always been a fascination of mine, because so many of the writers of that genre turn out to be true visionaries. It is as if they have actually seen the future, and come back to us to write about it.) One of the conventions of science fiction is that time travel is dangerous. Many writers feel that if you could fast-forward your life, the experiences you chose to live through would be empty, because you would not gain any emotional perspective along the way.

At this stage of my life (let's just say over 40, okay?), I have come to heartily believe that going against my instincts is a bad idea. The good news is that my instincts at this stage of my life are, more often than not, correct, whether I am embarking on a new venture or interviewing potential new hires for my clients. My point: Gut instinct is reliable, but it comes only as a result of experience.

So, if your gut instinct tells you that you probably are not going to make progress, move a conversation forward, or ultimately sell something to a given prospect, then the smart, professional, and nonjerk thing to do is to stop calling.

When someone calls on you repeatedly even though you haven't responded, encouraged, invited, or bought, your reaction is usually that he or she needs to get a clue. Don't you agree?

Applying Pressure

Applying pressure is similar to selling via fear. The key difference is that the reasons for the buyer to act vary.

In this regard, people who sell like a jerk use phrases like, "I have a quota to make," or "I wouldn't have come all the way here if I had known you were not ready to order." These, sadly, are too often used by salespeople trying to close a sale. Such statements may sound unbelievable, but I assure you there are salespeople out there right now using them.

Another point I want to make here is that being a salesperson does not wash away personality traits and tendencies; if anything, it *amplifies* them. I say this to encourage you to examine honestly how you want to be perceived, accepted, and endorsed. When I started in sales, I was a highly impatient individual. This has mellowed over the course of time. I am proud of that statement—not only because it is true but also because I believe that the strengths of my personality became enhanced as I learned to sell successfully, after having been turned down numerous times. Patience is important to me, which does not mean that practicing it has ever been easy.

Some Parallels

Much like closing a sale, playing a musical instrument demands patience, diligence, and discipline. Learning to play in time and in tune, and in synch with other musicians at all levels of competency, creativity, and proficiency requires a lot of patience. If you are not a musician, or have never practiced an instrument, you might instead think of it as learning to play golf. Or compare it to being a good parent. Patience is not something you switch on and off. Like any valuable currency, it is learned and earned.

Applying pressure to close a sale indicates that you do not care about the people you are selling to, or their business, or their profitability, or—worst of all—whether they ever buy from you again. Be patient. Be professional—don't sell like a jerk.

Being Rude

Well, let's see . . . where are there examples of rudeness in today's society? A pervasive example, is having someone standing behind you (in line at the supermarket, or waiting to board a plane) speaking as loudly as he or she possibly can into a cell phone, so that you and everyone within earshot becomes an unwilling participant in the conversation. That's rude. Equally rude is talking loudly in a movie theater. (This drives my son, a film editor and rabid cinema fan, crazy.) People act as though they are watching the film in their own living rooms.

When a salesperson calls on companies, hoping to do business with them, but fails to behave with a modicum of respect or comportment, he or she can expect to be shut down faster than an illegal dogfight at a famous athlete's home.

Examples of rudeness in the sales profession include cutting off a prospect when he or she is speaking, refusing to take no for an answer, and talking down to an employee or coworker.

Taking All the Credit

Salespeople sometimes believe that they are the center of the universe. I applaud this thinking, because when you are the center of the universe, you have no doubt about what you are doing. When you are the center of the universe, you assume everyone will want to talk to you.

Selling is not a solitary profession. Rarely (if ever) does the seller design, build, manufacture, erect, deliver, or install what is sold. When something (a product, service, or idea) is sold, that event triggers a wide range of other activities, providing other people with work and attention, and it is a good reminder to us sellers that we may NOT be the center of the universe!

One great benefit of the "center of the universe" perspective does empower sales people to boldly pick up the phone or walk into a place of business with the assumption that there is an opportunity there with their name on it.

I do not want to sell to everyone. I have really thought this through. First, I don't have that kind of time. Second, I want to be choosy about whom I do business with. I would much rather sell to people who will invite me back; moreover, often those are the people I get along with. We talk about things other than the dollar amount of the deal.

I want people to buy from me more than once. Although statistics may be suspect (80 percent of them are fabricated, according to something I wrote earlier in this book), it takes three times as much time, effort, resources, and money to win a new client or customer as it does to sell repeatedly to an existing one.

We must keep in mind that although we feel as though we are unique and sometimes very powerful as salespeople, we are part of a great economic machine. Jerks take all the credit for things that they only partially contributed to. This is not a good practice.

Refusing to Admit to Their Own Errors

One way that most people can sense a jerk mentality is that no matter what goes wrong (delivery, billing, correct fulfillment of an order or request) the sales person can tell you who is to blame, how that person is unreliable, or how their employer is struggling with some vague issue.

The nonjerk, professional seller takes full responsibility for anything that happens, whether they are the cause, or know the cause, or saw the cause coming up the street and tried to avoid it.

Now that we have covered some "don't do this" type of instructional ground, it is time for you and I to begin to dig into the meat of what has provided me with a fun, exciting, and powerfully useful way of making a living for the past nine years.

I have been fortunate enough to break down an approach to the conversation section of a sale to a process that has made a huge difference in people's selling lives for many years.

Moving Conversations Forward™ is a specific, acquirable skill that turns traditionalist selling techniques and approaches on their ear.

Sales people have been doing the same thing for 4,000 years, and this just may be the culmination of how the next 4,000 years of selling can be a different experience for both sellers and buyers.

As you read Chapter Four, it will be interesting to see if you see this *Moving Conversations Forward* approach as something you can apply and use both within traditional sales calls, as well as during conversations with friends, loved ones, and golf partners.

See you in Chapter Four!

Painfully True Selling Story # 3

I went to call on a manager at RR Donnelly on Park Avenue in New York, to sell our temporary staffing services. It turned out she had just moved to town with her significant other. She and I really hit it off during the meeting, so I felt very comfortable with this person whom I had just met.

At one point, she said, "Phil, you seem like a sophisticated guy, can I ask you a question?"

Hoping that it would not be anything too personal or inappropriate, I told her to fire away. Her question was: "My boyfriend and I are looking for a vacation destination in the Caribbean; can you help us?"

I said, "I have been to more than 20 islands and would be happy to share my knowledge."

She said: "What do you think of Aruba?"

Now, as a sales manager who trains salespeople before, during, and after presentations, to perform complete discovery by asking open-ended questions, I *should* have asked: "Why do you ask about Aruba?"

Instead, I jumped in and said: "Aruba might be my least favorite island. It is flat with sparse vegetation. The hotels look like old versions of Miami Beach hotels and there is usually an ugly oil tanker spoiling your view of the horizon. Why did you ask about Aruba?"

Her response: "My boyfriend and I love Aruba! It's our favorite island; we have been there five times."

End Result: I was unable to extract my foot from my mouth. I lost the sale—and could never get business from her. It was an invaluable lesson, and I tell the story to all my sales trainees.

—Phil Jakeway
President
The Supporting Cast

CHAPTER FOUR

MOVING CONVERSATIONS FORWARD

At every stage of a relationship, and at every stage of a sales call, it is essential that the conversation continuously move *forward*. This is particularly relevant to, and resonant within, productive sales conversations. When I began using the phrase: "Moving Conversations Forward™," everyone I encountered between the ages of 19 and 90 readily identified with the concept. It struck me as elegant, and unique, and so I applied to the U.S. Trademark office for ownership and protection of the phrase.

We all want conversations to move forward but, often, a distraction, lack of focus, or even lack of skill prevents us from achieving this simple and honorable goal. Moving Conversations Forward is the single most important skill to develop if you want to sell without being a jerk. It is a

considerate, common-sense approach to engaging in conversations, and it immediately removes any impression the
prospect may have that you are overbearing, belligerent, or
annoying.

Moving Conversations Forward is also a process, a
straightforward one, that I have taught and coached for over
15 years, and now I introduce you to it here, in book form.

THE PROCESS

In any conversation, there is some semblance of what I refer
to as "cosmic momentum," which I introduced in Chapter
Two.

No doubt you've heard Isaac Newton's three laws of motion, the first of which is: An object in motion tends to stay
in motion unless acted upon by an external force. I've para-
phrased that for the purpose of this discussion: Conversations at rest tend to stay at rest; conversations in motion
tend to stay in motion. To keep conversations in motion (and
commission rates paid), salespeople must give them regular
nudges and take action steps so they acquire momentum,
motion, and forward progress. Conversations in motion remain in motion only when they are "fed" in the right way,
with the right intentions.

Let's agree (for the boundaries of this book, and the ongoing use of these ideas in your life) that our definition of
SELLING is: "Having people feel good about making a positive decision to Move the Conversation Forward with me,
today." As such, we have a platform and frame of reference
from which to continue. Simply stated, any conversation
that has motion is one where there has been a "touch," some

contact or conversation between you and the other person. Any and all connections that have brought the two of you into direct contact count as a touch. For example, let's say you, the salesperson, and I, the prospect, met at a networking function, a charity fund-raiser, or at my office (where you cold-called). Regardless of where the initial contact was made, you are now in a position to Move the Conversation Forward. It is up to you to see if you can develop a favorable situation in which we might do just that.

Forward motion in conversation is a powerful thing, and anyone who wants to sell without being a jerk and generate forward motion in conversations looks forward to the next contact, or touch. If you have spoken with a prospect at least one time before, it is up to you to initiate the next contact or touch, and prepare to conduct the conversation according to a basic, yet profound and reliable three-step outline:

1. Review the past.
2. Discuss their (the prospects') present.
3. Plan the future TWOgether (misspelled on purpose, to ensure that it makes a mental impression with you).

Let's break each step down, and discuss the logic and thinking behind it, along with the emotional opportunity each offers to get people to buy from you on a regular basis—ideally, for the rest of your working life.

Review the Past

Within 15 seconds, you, as the person initiating the call or conversation, must bring a prospect up to speed on the what, where, how, or why (or any combination of these) that brought you together in the first place.

Also in that 15-second window, you must identify a few things to help your prospect understand the purpose of the conversation. Here's an example:

> "Hi, Reader [that's what I call you in my mind], this is John Klymshyn calling, from the Business Generator. You and I spoke about [insert time frame—a week, a few weeks, etc.] ago, and at that time you mentioned to me that you were considering different vendors for [describe your offer here].
>
>   How's my timing, for you and I to speak for a few minutes?"

I accomplished many things in this short, pointed, and powerful statement; but it's the last thing I said that is so important I want to point it out first. After I made a statement, I asked a question. Not only a question, but a *Million-Dollar Question.*

Note

I discuss Million-Dollar Questions and how to create them in Chapter Six.

This specific structured improvisational approach came out of my realization that you have to be able to engage and involve the people you call on in a way that is different from anyone else calling on that person, that day. Do not be naïve. The fact is that any decision maker in any organization has either just been called on or is about to be called on by another salesperson. He or she may not be selling what you sell, but that is not the point. You must differentiate yourself from anyone selling *anything*. I know that sounds like a big challenge, but so is selling without being a jerk.

The purpose of the first step in Moving Conversations Forward (Review the Past) is to bring the person you are calling into the frame of mind that returns him or her to your previous conversation. It reminds the suspect, prospect, or client about the previous connection you made, and it clears some mental space that enables the person to prepare for the next step of the conversation.

By reviewing the past, you also set a tempo for the rest of the call. By immediately following your statement with a question, you take control of the conversation from the outset.

Painful Selling Truth #7 applies here:

The first person to ask three questions in a row takes control of the conversation.

At this stage, you have asked only one question, but you have preempted questions from your prospect, by identifying yourself and your company and then reminding the person you have spoken before. Following those statements with a question like "How's my timing?" identifies you as someone who shows respect for another person's time.

Note

People are surprised when I tell them I view it as a positive reaction when a prospect says the timing is bad to talk. Why? Because it prompts me to move to the next logical question: "When would be a better time for us to speak?"

What follows is one of the great challenges for salespeople: *Stay quiet long enough for the prospect to think, and then deliver an answer.*

If I ask you a question and decide halfway through it that I would prefer to ask you another question, I might feel compelled to deliver the second question before you answer my first. This creates a quagmire, and is a form of verbal quicksand. It signals the beginning of a conversation spiraling out of control. Remember, the goal here is to move the conversation forward. We do not want to force, drag, drive, or push the conversation forward; we want to *move* it forward. This requires tenacity, patience, thought, and a sense of timing.

Keep in mind: Your calling me today *does not* translate to my wanting or needing to buy from you today.

If you can demonstrate to your prospects that you are willing to wait for the relationship to develop, and that the immediate sale is not your top priority, then you will build a long, fun, profitable career in sales. Think about it: You may meet or call on someone today to whom you could still be selling many years from now. This fact is exciting, but too often overlooked.

If the first step, Review the Past, results in an invitation to begin the process again at a later date, you have time to plan to accommodate that invitation. If, on the other hand, you luck into that rare experience of someone responding to your timing question with, "Yes, I have a few minutes now," you must be ready to act.

When your prospects grant you an audience with them on the spot, the next step requires that you do something very difficult, and it marks the turning point of moving away from traditional selling and toward selling without being a jerk.

Rather than launch into what you can offer them, you ask questions about them or their business in a noninvasive way. Your questions should prompt thought on the part of the person you are looking to engage. My goal is to control conversations, be persuasive, yet nonthreatening. By doing that, I get them thinking about (and getting ready to share with me) what is on their mind. That's the goal of step two: Discuss Their Present.

Discuss Their Present

You cannot know your prospects' present unless you *ask them about it.* The best way to get the information you need is to ask simple, direct questions to get them talking about what's going on with them right now. For example:

- "Where are you in that process today?"
- "What is the latest with that project?"
- "What has changed since the last time we spoke?"

Now, depending on your ability to listen and your desire to sell without being a jerk, you have an opportunity to set yourself apart from every other salesperson in the world. This is the stage of the conversation where you consciously implement a mathematical formula that was first developed to explain economics. An Italian by the name of Vilfredo Pareto devised what is now commonly referred to as the 80-20 Principle, which says that "80 percent of all events come from 20 percent of causes." The application of this ratio in sales is that our job, our responsibility, and our most reliable habit in being able to sell without being a jerk, by moving conversations forward, is to:

Listen 80%

Respond 20%

That's our job, our responsibility, and the magic bullet that will set us apart from our competition. Sounds simple, right? All you have to do is keep your information-rich, full-of-features-and-benefits mouth closed long enough to actually *hear* what the other person is saying, before you say anything!

I was introduced to this powerful and reliable concept when I went through the first real sales training I had ever received. Ironically, I had already been selling for about four years, and at the time was employed as a recruiter by an executive search firm in Encino, California. The office had a formal training system and, more importantly, a resident trainer named Sandy Smith. She impacted my life 17 years ago when she explained this life-changing, common-sense idea, which I still use, teach, and adhere to. What she said to me was:

"If you listen more than you talk, you achieve many things."

And if you listen more than you talk:

- People will think you are smart, because you listen well.
- People will be more comfortable speaking to you the third, eighteenth, and hundredth time.
- You actually will become smarter about what is going on with the people you call on, whether that is defined

by a vertical market, size of business, or a geographical area.

- You will not sell like a jerk because you will not be busy pitching or trying to convince those you talk *to* that they should buy from you.

Productive Perspective

If you view selling (in particular, selling without being a jerk) as a process, as opposed to an event, you will gain the perspective of duration, of productivity for the long term—that is, you will focus on length of relationships developed over multiple touches or interactions, over a period of time. Not years, not forever, but a period of time.

When someone says to me that the timing for this particular call is not great, I ask, "When would it more appropriate for us to talk?" Then I listen in *silence* for his or her answer. By doing this, I have begun to make an impression on them that other salespeople do not, because:

- I have shown respect for their time.

- I have demonstrated both patience and awareness that relationships require time and effort.

- Most importantly, I have not come across as a hard-sales, do-it-now-or-forget-it type of salesperson.

- In this way, selling parallels the development of other relationships.

Emotional Timing

Have you ever tried to take a relationship somewhere it is not ready to go? My daughter has a distinct way of expressing that uncomfortable, pressure-filled and distasteful experience. She says, simply, "Ewww!"

Having emotional timing means you recognize that other people's lives may be running at a different pace (and have a different focus) from yours when you choose to call on them.

I always keep my focus, and short-term goal clear: to *move the conversation forward*, so when a suspect, prospect, or client says to me "Why don't you call me next Wednesday?" my immediate, patient, and reasonable response is, "Great! Thanks. Bye!" He or she is interested in continuing with his or her workday, not in "blowing me off" or "stringing me along."

If there's one phrase I wish I could remove from the selling language, it would be "buyers are liars." I have heard this millions of times. It upsets me whenever anyone says it, but more so when said by someone with a limited amount of experience. To me, it means one thing: This is someone who does not want to go out and gather his or her own empirical data; he or she is listening to the people in the office or industry who want to keep as many competitors out of the market as possible. One way to achieve that is to promote gloom and doom.

Other distracting and useless (and yet popular) comments are: "The market is bad," "No one is looking to change," "It's not a good time to call on people," and other annoying statements. These are repeated in sales offices and on sales teams all across the country every day. I know because I have spent the last eight-plus years in sales offices in all fields, where I hear variations of these themes, regardless of the current state of the economy or the local market.

When someone responds to my Million-Dollar Question—"How's my timing?"—with an invitation to call another day, I have achieved my goal of moving the conversation forward. I have not closed a deal, or nailed down an appointment, or acquired an RFP. But I *have gotten* an invitation (when you say it, it is a fact) to the next step.

Every step in the sales process is an incremental step forward. And even tiny, forward-motion steps will add up, covering large chunks of real estate over time. Patience in the selling process is so important. Focus on the issue at hand. See where the conversation goes, as opposed to trying to force it down a particular path, at your speed, on your agenda.

When I do this with multiple contacts in my database, on my list, or in my territory, I start to generate momentum, and that momentum manifests in having more things to do, more conversations to manage, and more people to engage.

Recently, a colleague asked me how I make sure I do not have "too many clients." I had to suppress a laugh, because I have yet to get to the point where I have too many clients. Yes, I know what it is like to be close to capacity with my travel, seminar, and coaching schedule, but no matter how much business development work I do, I have never had to turn assignments away. Every client relationship has the potential to build, grow, and then fade. Not all do, but they have the potential to. This frees up my calendar to accommodate the next most active prospects, turn them into clients, and serve them.

I live to serve.

If you can sell to people without their feeling as though you are there to squeeze cash out of them, you will tend to be invited back (invitation versus permission). This prompts the achievement of the third step in the Moving Conversations Forward process, which is to *Plan the Future TWOgether*.

Plan the Future TWOgether

Yes, we all (me, my editor, my copy editor, and the marketing people who worked on this book) recognize that the above word is spelled incorrectly. It is a device, and it used on purpose, to ensure that it makes a mental impression with you.

When you and your prospect plan the future TWOgether, it implies that you have changed the dynamic of the typical seller/prospect conversation. Usually, seller/prospect conversations are seen as face-to-face exchanges, where the two parties confront each other—with the interaction bordering at times on the combative.

Instead, imagine being invited to stand elbow to elbow with your prospects as you both look down a path that the two of you will walk together. It may not be the path that you had in mind, but instead is defined by what the prospect says, not what you can suggest. We have to pay attention to what is going on. If someone knows who you are and what you do, and you call them, they know you are calling to see if you can sell them something. This is not a bad thing! We have to have the process in mind, and the next step of the process is where things get interesting. It is where there is a significant amount of risk, and as a result, an overwhelmingly high rate of reward.

Subtle Differences

Sometimes it's the subtle differences that can be the most profound. Consider that I did not title this book "The Only Effective Approach to Selling!" Or, "Forget Everything You Know about Selling!" I would be loath to buy a book that made those types of claims. But selling without being a jerk depends on you implementing a subtle difference in your approach, your stance, and your reactions to what you see, hear, and feel as a professional seller. If you have been selling for many years, this may be the turning point, when you move from being a steady, middle-of-the-road salesperson to being a top-flight producer. And if you are new to the game, this may help you understand why your friends and family raise their eyebrows when you tell them that you have accepted a position that is heavily sales oriented. Tell them that you are going to do your job just a little differently, and like the proverbial fork in the road, that subtle difference, that one choice, will make all the difference. You will succeed where others have failed.

In order to Plan the Future TWOgether, you must—you guessed it—ask questions. A sampling of those questions you might ask include:

- Where do we go from here?
- What would you like to see happen next?
- What is our best next step?
- How should I prepare for our next conversation?

That last point raises an important issue—that conversations should be *conversational*. I find it fascinating that salespeople often seem to believe that sales conversations should be conducted differently from other kinds of conversations. Why? In general, I think it's because they have trouble with standard conversations because they feel that they should have a specific measurable agenda and result; and they have trouble with sales conversations because they do not know how to convince prospects to adhere to a specific, measurable agenda, leading to a specific, measurable result.

Avoid Yes/No Questions

In my training sessions, I ask salespeople to gather in groups to cold-call each other. There is only one rule: If anyone asks a yes or no question, the answer he or she receives must be a no. I have them do this to break the habit most people have of asking yes or no questions, and to open their minds to the exciting possibilities offered by asking open-ended questions—in other words, questions to which they do not know the answer.

The fun begins when I ask these groups of salespeople to find out three things about the others in their group. I give them 30 seconds to do this. Next I ask them to cold-call each other again. Inevitably, the second round of cold calling takes them much further. Why? Because (as is usually pointed out by one of the participants), when they conduct the conversations without a specific agenda (e.g., I want an appointment with this prospect, or I have to quote a special to this prospect) they are more relaxed, and the conversation is much more, well, conversational.

Remember, every selling conversation is, by definition, a conversation—nothing more. It may lead to a negotiation, but that comes later. It may lead to a face-to-face appointment, but that, too, may come later.

If you are interested in selling without being a jerk, it means you will have to accept the challenge of doing things just a little bit differently from what you might have been taught or encouraged to do in the past.

REVIEW

Moving Conversations Forward means that you maintain an emotional distance from the specific occurrences on each call or conversation. There is no bad news or good news. There is only data, and your job is to gather all the data you can, then determine whether what you do, offer, or provide might be of use or value to the prospects you call on.

Isn't it a relief to learn that your suspicions have been validated? That selling can be done by people with good intentions, and that selling is honorable, and exciting, and profitable and fun?

Moving Conversations Forward is an art. It requires skill, a bit of discipline to practice and implement the skill, and it requires a bit of humility.

You do not have to pretend that you know everything. Not knowing everything is hardly the same as not knowing anything.

Be careful about what you say, promise, or infer. If you think you could save someone money by their deciding to buy from you, find a way for them to discover that without you stating it outright. If what you offer truly is better than what people are currently buying, then you should be able to relax, and do what makes selling so interesting to many people like me who have done it for an extended period of time: It is fascinating, because it is about people, it involves people, and we get to meet and engage people.

In order to sell without being a jerk, you have to have that "sense of human" I referred to, and that means that you can enjoy the difficult, exciting, and challenging work.

By continuing to follow the line of thought I am marching out in this insightful and entertaining little book, you and I have come to an agreement. You have decided at the very least, that what I espouse, and what I teach, resonates with you at one or more levels. Isn't it wonderful to discover that selling can be done more professionally, cordially, respectfully, and *successfully* than how many other philosophies encourage?

I love to sell, because I love hearing what people have to say.

I love to Move Conversations Forward, because it is *not* easy. And I love the fact that you are going to turn the page, and join me in the continuation of this overall conversation.

Painfully True Selling Story # 4

One thing that drives me *absolutely crazy* is talking with salespeople who never answer a question. Many salespeople in the commercial real-estate brokerage business and other service-related industries are trained to answer every question *with* a question.

This evasive approach to selling can often be maddening for a prospective tenant or purchaser.

Case in point:

Many years ago I had a listing with another broker in my office that was just such a salesperson. The listing was for a very old, complicated, and sizable industrial facility in central New Jersey.

One day we were showing the facility to a prospective buyer who was very detail oriented. As we conducted the tour, the prospective purchaser asked questions one after the other.

"How many parking spaces does the building have?" asked Mr. Prospect.

"How many do you *need*?" answered the broker.

"Two hundred and fifty," said the prospect. "No problem," said the broker.

"How high are the ceilings in this particular section?" asked Mr. Prospect.

"What sort of ceiling height do you need?" asked the broker.

"Sixteen feet clear," responded our prospective purchaser.

"That's what we have!" responded the broker.

"How deep are the loading dock wells?" asked Mr. Prospect.

"What sort of trucks do you get?" asked the broker.

"Straight trucks," said the prospect, appearing to lose patience.

"Perfect for straight trucks!" remarked the broker.

"Is the building on septic or sewer?" asked the prospect, visibly irritated.

"What's best for your operation?" said the broker.

At this point the prospect was clearly frustrated. He asked again in an impatient tone and the broker just looked at him. He obviously didn't know the answer.

"Let me ask it another way!" snapped the potential purchaser, "and please give me an *answer*, not a *question*!

"When you sit on the toilet and do your thing, where does it go when you flush?"

"It goes away," said the broker!

Hence, the showing came to an immediate end.

—Rick Marchisio
Executive Vice President
Managing Director
Grubb & Ellis Company
New Jersey

CHAPTER FIVE

PROCESS AND COMPLETION

Selling without being a jerk can be a tall order. It is not as easy as it sounds. It requires you to build the foundation of a relationship and to make sure that the structure of the conversation you have within the relationship is sound. It requires that any nervousness you may have about lack of production (any shortfall, at any time, for any reason) is never evident in your approach to the selling conversation.

YOUR QUOTA, YOUR PROBLEM

One undeniable fact about the selling life is that salespeople must be able to operate under pressure. They may not have to make decisions about national policy, or decide which family continues to receive benefits while another loses theirs, but selling is a very challenging profession.

Specifically, pressure in the selling profession is applied each week, month, or quarter by the requirement to meet *quota*, a beautiful little word that refers to the minimum required revenue production (weekly, monthly, or quarterly) they must achieve to keep their jobs. And though salespeople go into the profession knowing about quotas, many tend to spend more time moaning (a sales management euphemism for anything from mild complaining to ongoing "change the rules" campaigns) about how far away they are from reaching their quotas than working to meet them.

Often, salespeople try to make the discrepancy between their current attainment and the looming quota everyone else's problem. If you have ever been on the phone with a salesperson attempting to sell you something, and he or she tried to entice you to buy strictly on the grounds that your purchase would help him or her make quota you may have thought: "What a JERK!" Or maybe you yourself have been guilty of pressuring someone to buy on these grounds. If so, consider this your "cease and desist" order.

Meeting your quota is your problem, no one else's. Well, on second thought, it's also the problem of your manager. And the VP of sales. And the company president. And every vendor that sells anything to your company. So, on further examination, I must allow that many people—possibly whole departments—may be dependent upon you meeting your quota. The point is, whether or not you reach your quota will have a ripple effect that can be felt by the whole company. Your quota is a contract you have entered into willingly, and the fact that you show up to work at a sales desk every day tells the world that you accept the challenge of finding a way to make quota this month, and every month.

Here is where that process becomes interesting: You want to sell without being a jerk. Presumably, your employer would support this as a course of action. Rarely do leaders in sales organizations get up in the morning thinking, "I wonder how much of a jerk my salespeople can be to our customers today." Of course, that's ludicrous!

Yet the pressure persists. I can say with full confidence that the most reliable cure for quota pressure is production. *Closed deals have a beautiful aroma.* Revenue is a great tool for winning the favor of your boss.

The first step to making production consistent and removing the "problem" sensation associated with quota is activity!

To sell without being a jerk is to generate *activity*. Activity refers to phone calls, visits, mailings, email blast marketing, newsletters, personal notes, walk-in sales appointments, canvassing, cold calls—anything that can be counted or measured. If what you do cannot be measured, there will be no way for you to improve it. If you make five calls and get no response, it does not mean that no one is buying; it means that you have not generated enough activity to find the people who are or who might buy soon.

Activity is the precursor to success, and it is the thing that most salespeople work hard to avoid. When they stop avoiding it, and generate it regularly, they outpace their peers, they out perform their competitors, and they enjoy reliable production—the Holy Grail of a successful sales career. Selling without being a jerk is dependent upon your ability and willingness to take responsibility for the consequences of your actions (*or inactions*). Activity also precludes you from the time-killing, unprofitable water cooler conversations that distract talented salespeople.

Specific Directed Activity

Specific directed activity is at the heart of this chapter. It is the reason that some salespeople look relaxed and confident the day before the end of the selling period. Conversely, it is the reason salespeople who avoid activity find that they need to create a flurry of it the night before the end of the selling period. Specific directed activity is about setting, then living out, priorities. It is about focus, and it is about discipline.

I attribute over 65 percent of my success as an entrepreneur (nine years and counting) to my ability to maintain a disciplined approach to sales. Translation: I generate activity on a regular, focused, and disciplined basis. In this chapter, not only will I give you reasons to do this, I will also tell you about simple, direct ways to impact your selling day—starting tomorrow. How does that sound?

Before I go on, though, I want to be absolutely clear: *Nothing* takes the place of activity. Not your personality, not your shiny shoes, not the contacts your dad introduces you to at the club. Nothing takes the place of activity.

The Value of Generating Activity

Generating activity solves multiple problems:

- It shows your boss or supervisor that you are actually trying.
- It removes a lot of fear and worry at the end of the month or end of the quarter, because nothing is more

powerful or more reliable for the person who wants to sell without being a jerk than having a lot of prospects and clients in the queue who might buy something at some later date. At every turn in my professional career, the end of the month, quarter, or contest period came with lightning speed. I was (and still am) determined to be ready for it.

- It lightens the load of emotional baggage that you might be carrying to work every day. No more dire thoughts such as, "I have to close this sale, otherwise my month is *shot*." If you have been selling for any period of time, you are familiar with this near-desperate feeling.

In my experience, whenever I lose discipline and allow myself to avoid generating activity, I start to get nervous. Maybe part of it is my guilt (based on a specific religious upbringing, which at my current stage of life appears to be built on a steady diet of fear and guilt, but that particular portion of my therapy we will save for another book)... I get nervous because I am not confident about where the revenue is going to come from down the road. It is my responsibility to build a compelling future for myself. It is my responsibility to front-load every selling month. It's yours, too.

I want to highlight that last thought, and camp out on it for a few paragraphs.

To increase your chances of meeting your quota every month, you must *front-load* every selling every month. I learned this technique while working as a recruiter for the United States Naval Reserve. In that position, I was measured by my percentage of attainment relative to a specific quota, much like a sales job. Likewise, I was measured by the calendar month, and the quarter, sort of like a sales job.

What was unique about that position was the reward for overachievement. In a sales position, you are rewarded with cash or services-in-kind (a weekend at a great hotel or something similar). Overachievement in the Naval Reserve netted me an additional star on my recruiting badge, and I filled all of the places stars could fit onto that badge. The accolades felt good, but they didn't earn me the key thing every sales person craves: cash bonuses!

So, I admit to sandbagging—saving closed deals for the next calendar month, in order to regularly achieve quota. I'm not proud of this, but I freely admit it.

My monthly assigned goal was seven qualified enlistments. To be considered a qualified enlistment, the person had to perform a job that my local divisions and battalions needed; had to be eligible for enlistment; and had to be physically fit, according to the U.S. Naval Reserve's standards for body fat percentage, and be able to pass a test of endurance and strength. I did well as a recruiter. I wore the uniform proudly, and I put a lot of people in the reserves. But at first, it was far from easy. People would not fully disclose disqualifying details until the day of enlistment or, worse, the week after. That meant that I would have to remove that enlistment from my count for the month. Every month, regardless of holidays, birthdays, sick days, vacation days, or snow days, the Naval Reserve needed seven new bodies in the program from me. In order to reliably make quota (and often exceed it) I would always look for just one more enlistment.

My mantra: Get 'em in early, get 'em in queue, and get 'em in the Navy!

The Calendar Is Moving toward You

It's the same for you. Every day of your career, your employer needs production from you. To meet that production requirement, front-loading and building future months' production is essential. Face it, if you plan on remaining in this profession, you will forever be accountable to the end of every month, or quarter, or whatever period you are measured for—for staying one step ahead of that moving calendar. Remember, you have a defined and consistent sales cycle, and although you may do some cold-calling today, it may not net you business today. Here's Painful Selling Truth #8:

If you want new business today, today is far too late for you to start working on it.

You know it is going to take some period of time between when you begin a conversation (a cold call, referral, networking contact, in-bound lead) and when a sale is likely to be made. If you allow longer than a week to pass between initial contact and the closing of the deal, you will have to overcompensate for any potential lapses in communication. The only reliable "shoring tool" I know is *activity*. Pick up the phone. Go to a meeting that you might have been on the fence about. Follow up on a new lead. *Do something*!

As Teddy Roosevelt's father is famous for saying, "Get action!" This was his cure for any and all ills. In his time, being idle was an illness. Imagine that!

I rely on a straightforward formula that helps me prepare sales activity, and which helps me to produce revenue on a regular basis.

Here it is:

Process + Patience = Production

When you have a process to manage (the one outlined throughout this book would be a good one to start with) and you employ patience, production is certain to follow.

Another method I recommend to help you manage pressure, increase enjoyment of the process, and aid in filling your quota is to organize your activities. By employing measurement tools to keep track of what you are doing, who you are calling on, and what you have done regarding a particular person, firm, organization, or company, you can increase your confidence in the fact that you are talking to the right person, about the right issue, at the appropriate stage in the selling conversation. This will give you a clear perspective of where you are in reaching your goals every month, as well as provide a reliable way of referencing and recognizing how much more you need to do.

I'm a fan of GOLDMINE software for organizing sales activity. This contact management software program offers a lot of cool personalization options; but the thing I like most about it is that it prompts you to think about each conversation as a part of the larger process. It gives you an accurate picture (based on your own input) and a patient perspective regarding the gestation of an overall conversation.

By adopting a reliable way of organizing your efforts, you take some of the uncertainty and anxiety out of selling, and you set a standard for yourself.

CONTAGIOUS ENTHUSIASM

When things are going well, you feel unstoppable, and you can enjoy the processes you are employing. To avoid (or prevent entirely) dark nights of the soul from occurring as part of the selling experience, you have to plan ahead.

Planning ahead means taking time to imagine what you want each new sales day to look like. Here's a great, simple way to do that. Take control of tomorrow's activity today.

With so much riding on emotion and response time in selling conversations, the combination of using contact management software and employing a specific call strategy, there is no limit to the level of success you can achieve. However, this only looks simple, because it is on paper, but believe me, if you think that you can just sit down, start dialing, and that there will not be a single attempted interruption, you are in for a surprise!

For example, no doubt you are familiar with the "lunchroom leftovers" scenario. Food fascinates, energizes, and most importantly; attracts salespeople. If you place food of any sort (sandwiches, pizza, salads) in the kitchen or conference room, and no one admonishes, "This is for a meeting," it will disappear as if starving hordes had invaded the place. Everyone will start talking about the food; most importantly, they will stop selling. This is a recurring nightmare of mine, and probably of most sales managers! It's just one of those things that we can always count on, things that are so reliable that we start to think that their *absence* would be a sign of the Apocalypse. Dogs barking when you are trying to get to sleep. Checks arriving four to thirteen days after you expected them. Bread landing on the floor, buttered-side down. Now, I am not a pessimist. Ask anyone who knows me. You can also ask them if they have that money they owe me, but that is a separate conversation altogether! But the premise is valid.

Another phenomenon you can count on for interruption is that people in office environments like to socialize. They want their cubicle to be the place where everyone goes for gossip, television reviews, or ideas on how early everyone can get out of the building on Friday. Unfortunately, if your cube is the gathering place, it is also a wasteland, the place people go to stand around and be unproductive—that is, to stop selling.

ENTER THE 20 CALL BURST

In all humility, I will tell you that the 20 Call Burst™ is the single greatest, most reliable self-disciplinary tool to impact sales effectiveness, reliability, and measurement since the invention of the telephone. This is an activity management solution that has been adopted in multiple industries, with profound results. Why? Because it prevents people from selling like a jerk.

First, the *How*

Take a look at any tool you use to track future conversations. Those tools should give you a list of people to reach out to, via the phone. (Tomorrow, later this week, and next month are all in the future, so those lists would be a perfect starting point.) Without counting them all up, start writing down the names and numbers of the people you would like to speak to tomorrow. I use the phrase "like to speak to" because you and I know that if you dial a prospect, there is no guarantee that you and the person will actually speak.

Now, start a new list. Stop when you have 20 people. Look at it and determine whether three or four of them can wait one more day to hear from you. If so, replace them with the names and numbers of people you have been meaning to cold-call.

Before you begin calling, however, you must commit to a calling period *without interruption*. That means not getting up, logging on to the Internet, chatting with a colleague, checking your cell phone for messages, or checking your email. You also will not take incoming calls during this period. This may sound outrageous. It absolutely IS outrageous how unfocused and undisciplined so many salespeople in the world are, and how many of them whine and complain that they cannot make quota, or bonus, or to the next level of commission percentages.

Focus, discipline, sense of humor: These are the distinguishing characteristics that separate average salespeople from great salespeople.

- Great salespeople provide regular, clean, and honorable profit for their employer.
- Great salespeople love what they do.
- Great salespeople sell without being a jerk.

The *Why* (I promised it, right?)

Using the 20 Call Burst approach is the primary activity that will give you the advantage over your competitors. It is the activity that will set you apart from your time-wasting office mates. And it is the activity that will clear your deck of all excuses and distractions. The 20 Call Burst adds a vital component to how you run your business: a net-effect momentum.

Remember I've said that momentum is a cosmic concept. It is difficult to measure, yet easy to recognize. It also can be difficult to create, and a challenge to maintain. But the wonderfully reliable aspect of momentum is that it feels goooooood!

The strength and reliability of the structure of your selling approach is well served by the powerful combination of activity and momentum.

Build and conduct 20 Call Bursts daily: Please say this sentence aloud. Do it again before you get out of your car or off the train tomorrow. Say it before you leave your house. And after you eat your lunch.

Why? Because contact management is essential to being able to sell without being a jerk. Contact management is not about bells and whistles; it is about having practical access to details, as well as a running record of the overall conversation with your prospects and clients. Once you have a good contact manager in place, you are firmly positioned to generate and maintain momentum.

How do I know this? Because I have had people call on me who did not have their notes and records in order, and I make life a living hell for anyone who calls on me, because I am a sales trainer, because I think they should be able to keep up with me, and because I want to make sure that only the best and the brightest refer to themselves as a practitioner of my profession.

The first and consistent emotional experience you want to have each selling day is *momentum*. Momentum will win you business. It will remind you, over time, of how important activity is. Momentum creates a sensation of abundance. The salesperson who regularly, and in disciplined fashion, goes out looking or business is bound to find some, and find it often—possibly every month.

The opposite experience is one of lack. You lack "juice" that momentum provides. You lack confidence, because you do not have many activities, as well as the lack of contacts and conversations in the queue for next month, the lack of commissions this month, or the lack of a sense of hope for the future. Lack can be erased with the simple introduction of momentum. Momentum is so powerful that I marvel at how often salespeople allow it to slip away.

Momentum is the nectar of the sales life, and yet we sales-people tend to turn our attention to other more glamorous aspects or immediately intriguing activities than getting on the phone and qualifying a database. The emotional trifecta of: (1) a qualified prospect, (2) an imminent need, and (3) a proclivity on the part of the prospect to buy from you can be overwhelming, not unlike a ride on a super-fast roller coaster. It is impossible not to get caught up in that, and forget for a moment the plodding, effort-laden activity of working through a list of prospects, getting someone to answer the phone, and hopefully put you in contact with a decision maker. It may not be as immediately rewarding, but it is essential.

I repeat: the 20 Call Burst is an activity that will turn your production (and sense of future) from barren and hopeless to optimistic and plentiful.

As I was preparing my previous book, *The Ultimate Sales Managers' Guide,* for final editing, I spoke with a manager I had known for some time. I asked him what he felt managers were most responsible for.

"You have to give your people hope!" he said.

If you don't have a manager who thinks like this man, you need to get this message: Salespeople live on hope, like the rest of the population lives on oxygen, and if you are not receiving hope from somewhere, you must create it yourself.

If it is your perception that the market, the economy, the current state of affairs in countries thousands of miles away are impacting your selling productivity, then think of the 20 Call Burst as a combination of a call to action and an answer to your prayers.

You are the most reliable source of motivation for yourself. You are the one who has to sit at your desk and rationalize and process whatever production you finished last month with. You are the one who will ultimately decide whether you are committed to your employer and to this exciting profession.

Another simple (yet elegant and reliable) formula: How + Why = Stunning Results.

When you understand *why* a 20 Call Burst is a good idea, and a better practice, and a great habit, then you add the fact that you now understand *how* to do it, you will experience stunning results.

We salespeople (yes, I always include myself in that group, because selling is at the heart of what I do) are our own worst enemy. We allow distractions and useless opinions to get in the way of us producing. When someone in our office, or on our team creates great results, others sit and wonder how they did it.

I say that it is straightforward, and not all that mysterious: They generated activity, the moved conversations forward, and they minimized their tendency to allow distractions to keep them from being productive.

Now that we have a clear picture of *how* and *why*, let's take one step back, and plan a 20 Call Burst in advance.

PLANNING A 20 CALL BURST

If you are committed to your employer and this profession, then I encourage you to plan a 20 Call Burst for your next selling day *right now*. Remember, the 20 Call Burst is an activity planning management and execution tool. It will allow you to clear your desk of pending conversations, it will enable you to build momentum, and it will free up time you did not realize you had.

Processes create production!

Start by totaling all of the people who are in current conversation with you about potential future business. Add a few cold calls—but I caution you to avoid making the entire 20 Call Burst a cold-calling exercise.

More on the process in a moment; first a few cautionary words.

Mathematically speaking, the 20 Call Burst is a sound principle because it does not waver. You either complete 20 dials in a row or you don't—$0 + 0 = 0$. You can spend the afternoon at the water cooler discussing "the one that got away" or you can build an income for yourself that will serve you for a long time. Every waking moment that you invest in mundane conversations and inanities, in general, is time you will never retrieve from the continuum. Don't shortchange your future by killing time with the office losers. Many sales teams have members who don't really care about quota or the profession. They just want a place to go every day. If they make quota every so often, and get to go to an office that has free coffee and people to talk to all day, they will remain as hangers-on. These people would love to take your time away from productive activities, because they are not interested in making salesperson of the month—and they really would prefer that you not make it either.

Don't let anyone in your office cost you income. Be polite, but be firm. Do what many of my coaching clients have done: Print out a sign that reads: "20 Call Burst—Go away!" Hang it where commission killers, enthusiasm assassins, and revenue ruiners can readily view it as they approach your desk. Politely wave to these folks as you continue to talk on the phone to prospects who want to spend money with you.

Let's Get to Work!

The 20 Call Burst technique requires advance preparation, but that is part of what makes the process so powerful. By preparing in advance, you are putting time to good use by mulling over a list of different prospects *before* you call them. Write down the names of the first 10 or 15 people you plan to call the following day.

Look at it this way: If you are a golfer, you know that you have multiple aspects and characteristics to your swing. You take a certain amount of practice swings before you actually step up to the tee. Why? Because it prepares you physically and mentally. It helps you focus your mind, and it allows your body to become accustomed to the demands you are about to put on it.

It also provides you with a clearer perspective. No one expects to hit that stupid little white ball perfectly every time do they?

A Word about Golf

Golf to me and my friends is an acronym that stands for good old laughter and fun. I use this analogy to golf here because if you have ever tried to use one of those clubs to hit one of those balls in just the right spot so that it goes to just the right place on the grass ... well, then you know how important preparation is.

I used to play golf. I played with my father's clubs after he passed away many years ago, partly as homage to him (he loved the game) and partly because I was curious about why he found it so captivating.

I say I *used* to play, because I was one of those guys out on the course looking more for a few laughs than an infinitesimal score.

> I respect everyone who takes the game seriously, and I respect those among them who also can have a great time while playing well; but I could not find a way to combine those two experiences, so I stopped playing.
>
> That said, one of my favorite rules of etiquette was created on the golf course by me and my friends:
>
> "It is not appropriate to talk *to* a golfer who is about to swing, but you may talk loudly *about* him."

OK, back to work.

Once you have built a 20 Call Burst (i.e., you have the names and the phone numbers of the 20 prospective companies you want to call), it is time to begin the process that will change your selling life experience forever.

Sit at your desk and set your phone to "do not disturb." Doing this prevents you from reading the caller ID to see whether the incoming call is more important than the outgoing one you would prefer to avoid. Any incoming calls may be returned at the beginning of your next 20 Call Burst. Next, close all Internet browsers and your email window. Yes, *close* them. Now turn on or open your contact manager, to begin your calling.

This is a discipline exercise, which implies that you may feel a sense of sacrifice attendant with it. Remember what I said earlier in this chapter: Nothing takes the place of activity.

During this calling period, making yourself unavailable to prospects, clients, your cat's veterinarian, or your friend's latest amazing discovery on YouTube *will not* prevent you from earning a living. The idea is to *choose* how you spend your time throughout the business day. I have done this for a long time. I still do.

Tip

Make sure your voicemail message indicates how long you will be unavailable so that when a buying customer calls, he or she knows approximately when you will return the call.

When I ran a team that sold print advertising to a very demanding clientele in southern California, my reps had a fit when I told them not to answer incoming calls during their 20 Call Burst periods. Their collective objection was, "But I will lose orders! My customers need me when they call, or they will go somewhere else!" Well, a small number of those customers did go somewhere else, and that is not an easy thing for a sales rep or a sales manager to accept. Over time, we did lose a few individual orders, but we did NOT lose any good (profitable) customers. Business people understand that there is more going on in your world than one phone call between you and them. I want you to be responsive, and available, but I also want you to balance that with the fact that as a sales professional, you must do the necessary, plodding, difficult work of moving multiple conversations forward each and every business day. If someone who buys from you learns that you are unavailable but only for a specific period of time, you would be hard pressed to convince me that you will lose that customer forever.

In addition, the more we insist that we must be available to people, the less control we are allowing ourselves to have over our business day. You being in a meeting for an hour is an acceptable, generally standard reason to not answer your phone. Calling someone back within the hour is responsive, and professional, and it will help you in the long run to write more business. (Close more deals, gain more customers, MAKE MORE MONEY.)

So, after a brief period of low level revolt, and severe discomfort on the part of the reps, they noticed that they felt less stress upon completion of a 20 Call Burst, for several reasons:

- They were focusing on a task they knew they should be doing, but had been successfully avoiding.

- When they were done, they knew that 20 people had heard their names, and the name of our company. Multiply that by how many reps or salespeople are in your office. That's how powerful this process can be.

- They were ready for whatever was next on their task list for the day. Completing the 20 Call Burst cleared their head, prepared them for other activities, (and there are many! Salespeople have to respond to email, put mailings together, check order status for existing clients, interact with customer support, track down answers and responses that are impeding a deal, and so much more. Salespeople want to try to do several things at once, yet they expect to complete those several items with proficiency and efficiency. Here's a question: "Do you get dressed in the shower?" If not, then you have a perfectly logical reason: You are doing one thing at a time, and then moving on to the next. Why not apply that philosophy to the very important work you have in front of you every day as a representative of your company, and this profession? My reps told me that once they understood (meaning they got it, did it, and habitually practiced it), it made them feel better about what they had accomplished on a given sales day.

I currently have a wonderful assistant by the name of Taryn Burns. She is a dynamo—smart, funny, and hard-working. She makes sure our clients are satisfied, and that they receive the attention they are due. If you were to ask her what our task completion mantra is in the office, she would most likely tell you, "We are not interested in speed; we are interested in accuracy!"

Accurate completion of your selling tasks throughout your selling day will assure you will close more sales. Take one task, work through to its completion, and move on to the next. I don't live to work; I work to live. I believe the 20 Call Burst will allow you the same luxury.

Doing one thing at a time, being focused upon that task, and then having a sense of completion when the task is done is good for the mind and the soul. It makes you feel as though you could actually explain to someone else what you did all day, if they happen to ask you over dinner.

Too often, we rush through the thunder and rush of our day, and wonder what exactly we accomplished. I don't like that feeling. If you don't either, I invite you to take a specific directed activity approach to selling tomorrow, and for the rest of your selling life.

I have had salespeople work for me who were not the most gregarious, nor the quickest with a witty comeback for a sarcastic remark, but they were people who could manage a process, and those were the folks that I knew would increase their income each year, and every year.

I have had the most highly confident people in the group come to me, and ask how a certain person was "really" getting all the deals they were writing up. I pointed them to the exact ideas, expectations and processes being outlined here in black and white for you.

Adopt the 20 Call Burst. Move Conversations Forward. You will make more money, and that's a fact.

To take all of these ideas, and bring them to a new and exciting level of accomplishment, we are now going to turn our attention to the tools you will need to engage people in conversations, so you can be invited to the next step.

You will accomplish this by learning, practicing, and eventually mastering what is outlined in the next chapter, where I offer you Million-Dollar Questions.

Painfully True Selling Story # 5

It was June 1997 when I went on my first sales appointment alone. It was to sell a homeowner's insurance policy.

Thinking I knew all the answers, the fun was about to begin. I sat with the prospect at their dining room table and I began to explain their new policy.

As I was explaining, the questions started flying.

They asked questions such as, "Is *this* covered on the policy?" and "If *this* happens, are you sure it will be covered?"

I had no idea how to answer because I simply didn't know. Finally I said, "This is my first appointment alone, and I have no idea what I am doing! Can I borrow your phone?" I ended up calling another agent to have him explain the policy and answer all of their questions.

The painfully true (and valuable) lesson I learned that day was:

It pays to be honest.

Ten years later, those people are still with my agency.

—Ron Rooner
Farmers Insurance
Valencia, California

CHAPTER SIX

MILLION-DOLLAR QUESTIONS

Making a lot of money is a good thing. I want you to make as much money as you possibly can. That is the purpose of this book: to help you establish a reliable and comfortable income. Ultimately, however, you are the arbiter of how to balance your personal time and work time. You are the judge of what is appropriate for you in terms of goal setting and goal getting.

Note

For a more detailed conversation on this, and some really useful advice about setting and getting goals, refer to my book, *The Ultimate Sales Managers' Guide*. In it you will find quotes from some of the top minds in sales and sales management, explaining how they regularly master and achieve great things, year in, and year out.

MILLION-DOLLAR QUESTION FRAMEWORK

I have enjoyed a fascinating path to discovering, confirming, and teaching techniques for long-term sales success. Of all of the discoveries I have made regarding the way people think about, understand, and apply sales techniques, my absolute favorite is how they develop questions. The questions people ask (and the alternatives that occur only *after* a conversation has ended) provide constant fascination for me.

Over the past seven years, I have made an informal study of the best types of, structures of, and building blocks for questions. I can tell you unequivocally that the framework I am going to share with you in this chapter (and beyond) is the best I have encountered. I did not invent this process, I admit. I have borrowed ideas, styles, and formats from hundreds of sources and thousands of conversations, and learned from many, many attempts that went wrong. I fondly (and proudly) refer to this process as: Trial and Multiple Error!

What I arrived at from this "study" is a framework for building Million-Dollar Questions. I use the label "million-dollar questions" for a few reasons. First, even as I write this in late 2007, One Million Dollars still sounds like *a lot of money*. Second, it indicates how valuable I find them. Third, mastering them—not trying them tomorrow, measuring their effectiveness based on limited results, and moving on, but *mastering* them—just might help you *make* a million.

I will personally guarantee, right here in print, that you will earn more money than you are now by combining these questions with the techniques I describe elsewhere in this book. As a matter of fact, if you work these ideas into your selling life, and after 30 days see no improvement in your ability to move conversations forward, be a better cold caller, or increase your income, call my office (you'll find the number in the back of the book) and I will personally write you a check for the price you paid for this book.

The framework for building Million-Dollar Questions is essential. Notice that I use the word "building" when referring to inventing these questions on the fly. If you think about conversations and language in musical terms, as I do, then it is a reasonable extrapolation to view building Million-Dollar Questions as a jazz performance piece.

Jazz is highly improvisational. It is about the magical marriage of knowledge of your instrument, the joy found in playing along with other musicians, and the creativity that can emerge under pressure—at a moment's notice.

Many musicians (like me) are intimidated by jazz, because it requires superior musicianship, creativity, and an ability to "stretch out," to take on an 18- or 24-bar solo and maintain a theme, phrase, or pattern over the course of that section or segment of the piece being played.

I can sing and play drums at the same time. Effectively, that means I am doing five things at once. Nevertheless, I am still intimidated by what goes on in the mind and heart of a jazz musician. (That does not keep me from banging on my drums at any opportunity!)

I am listening to jazz while I write this, because it is just that inspiring to me. So, what does this have to do with building Million-Dollar Questions? The parallel is that sales occurs and functions within the framework of accepted business practices and conventions. Building Million-Dollar Questions is the 24-bar solo that occurs within the framework of the selling conversation. It requires that you improvise. The best improvistiaion is only possible when you are a disciplined and engaged listener. You must be aware of what is going on, where you might add, and where things might go, within the framework of the current experience.

How can you make a joyful and worthwhile contribution (as opposed to finding a way to show off or dominate the experience), if you are not listening, aware, and responsive?

Salespeople are similar to musicians in that we like to perform, and we like to participate. We are competitive, and yet we are fascinated when people who play a different instrument (or sell a non competing product) excel.

One of the great improvisational aspects and conventions of music is that you do not have to fill every space with a note or a riff. Likewise, salespeople do not have to be talking to Move Conversations Forward. Kind of convenient, isn't it? Well, I think so.

Musicians who "jam" enjoy what they do because it is a communal but fleeting experience. Salespeople who sell without being a jerk love building Million-Dollar Questions because it is so intensely cerebral.

A key cerebral and improvisational componenet to selling without being a jerk is building Million Dollar Questions. The questions you will learn, and learn to develop, in this chapter will open doors, create next steps, and help you increase your income in the short term and continue to increase it incrementally over the long term of your tenure in the greatest profession in the world.

But first, a definition: Million-Dollar Questions are short, pointed, inquiries used during a sales call. These questions are about the *other* person in the conversation and are used to get him or her thinking in a certain way or about a next step, which is absolutely essential to win a sale. These questions also help to continue and expand conversations, and, more importantly, evoke invitations.

I would rather receive an invitation to move forward than permission to meet with someone immediately. By working for, earning, and receiving invitations, rather than looking to close a quick sale, we effectively set ourselves apart from anyone else selling to that person today.

When you do not act like a jerk, but instead act like a friendly, genuinely interested human being, the people you sell to will be surprised and delighted. Think about it: People will probably buy something similar to what you have to offer at some point in time. There is no mystery there. The mystery lies in who will succeed in selling it to them. Will that person be you—or a jerk?

If you are the one to sell it, and you do so without resorting to being a jerk, the person buying will be relieved, thrilled, and satisfied that he or she bought it from you. And, chances are, you'll get an invitation to come back, which is the entire purpose and point, right?

Whenever there is a key opportunity to build, support, or finish the construction of a conversation, you may have an opportunity to deliver a Million-Dollar Question. By "deliver" I mean offer these questions as a means of learning about the other person. And note that no single question will be the magic bullet that will win you the sale or seal the deal. This is precisely the point behind the phrase and concept: Move Conversations Forward.

One more musical analogy: I cannot build a great break on the drums if I do not understand the time signature. If everyone is playing in 6/8 time, and I want to put in four beats and a crash, I might be ahead of the specific crescendo of the song we are playing. My point? In selling, as in music, it's about the timing.

FORMULATING MILLION-DOLLAR QUESTIONS

Before you can deliver Million-Dollar Questions, you must know how to formulate them. To begin formulating them, let's first identify the two necessary elements to all Million-Dollar Questions, the "Do's," and the "Don'ts."

The Do's comprise a list of simple ways to ask questions for which yes or no are not options for answers.

Do's

Who

What

When

Where

Why

How

Which

Examples:

- How are you? (versus: "Are you OK?")
- What's new? (versus: "Is anything new?")

Examples

Who, what, when, where, why, how, and which: When you begin questions with one of these, you are almost guaranteed to avoid the yes/no trap.

The don'ts are the words that you must avoid putting at the opening of your questions. The reason to avoid them is simple; applying it is not.

When you use one of the following to open your questions, you are doomed to receive a yes/no answer:

Can

Do

Is

Will

Should

Are

Have

Examples

- Question: Do you want me to call you later? Answer: *Uhhh...no, I don't.*

- Question: Can I send you information? Answer: *If you want.* Note: they may *say* yes, but that hardly creates an invitation to the next step. Remember: You mailing me something because you want to send it is not the same as me asking for it.

- Question: Is now a good time for us to talk? Answer: *Nope.*

If in reading these questions you found yourself cringing because you have heard them come out of your mouth recently, that's fine. It means that you have a gut instinct for the fact that you are digging yourself a hole when you ask these types of questions.

Here's an exercise. When you take a break from reading this book, go start a conversation with the person nearest to you (a flight attendant, your cubicle neighbor, a next-door neighbor...) and see how many questions you can ask without getting a yes or no answer.

OK—I assume you are back from that grueling exercise. Notice anything?

Most people find that they can ask only one or two Million-Dollar Questions before they default to asking the yes-or-no variety.

Now that we have started coming to an agreement about how valuable it can be to listen, ask a question based on what you heard, and then go on to the next step, let's take things to a more human level, with a much more unique approach.

In order to sell without being a jerk, we have to find a way to connect with people. This means that learning about them requires listening, and that Million-Dollar Questions can be used to get the suspect, prospect, client, boyfriend, or boss to tell us stuff that will help us to move the conversation forward.

As I mentioned earlier, this is highly cerebral, but the foundation is emotional.

As such, it is time to introduce to the Million-Dollar Question formula: the Emotional Trigger Word.

If people buy based on emotion (they do) and if they feel more comfortable when people let them talk (they most CERTAINLY do) then we have done some pretty sophisticated deduction to arrive at the fact that if I ask you questions about you, your business, or other things that you care about, then I have a chance (no guarantees, but a chance) at separating myself from every other competitive seller who calls on you, solely based on my ability to sell without being a jerk.

I hope your service or product is superior to whomever you compete with, but the reality is that your product or service may not stack up well against certain competitors. So, the advantage must lie in how well you sell.

It lies in your ability to ask questions that are short, elegant, clearly about the other person, AND that get them thinking in a way that no other person is getting them to think.

This is a huge undertaking. Do not take this lightly. Go get a highlighter, and start turning this copy of this book into your own source material for your Ph.D. in how to sell.

Emotional Trigger Words do exactly what their title suggests: They trigger emotions. This is not a design to control someone's mind—it is a way to get conversations moving, and moving smoothly.

Here is a short list of emotional trigger words:

Like	Think	Feel	Want	Agree
Need	Hope	Help	Wish	
Enjoy	Dislike	Believe		

These words get the real action going in Million-Dollar Questions.

Example:

> - What do you think?
>
> - How do you feel about that?
>
> - What do you believe would make sense to do next?
>
> - What would you like to see happen now?
>
> - What do you want to accomplish?
>
> - What help can our company offer you?
>
> Notice how I have avoided (yes, specifically avoided) adding "salesy" sounding statements that hint at "adding value," "removing pain," or "solving a problem."
>
> Although your product or service very well may do all of those things, it is much more powerful for a prospect to discover those facts on their own than for you to try to pitch them at every opportunity.
>
> Remember: When someone hears something come out of my mouth, they hear an opinion. When it comes out of their own mouth—it's a fact!

So, when we take a "do" and follow it with a "don't" and add an emotional trigger, we change the dynamic of the question. We change the number of responses we can receive from two (yes or no) to several hundred thousand, and we are now on a unique and exciting path to controlling conversations and being persuasive, yet nonthreatetning.

Now, here are some of my favorite Million-Dollar Questions. Their simplicity may surprise (and, I hope, delight) you.

- How does that sound to you?

- What do you think of what we have discussed so far?

- What do you like most about what you do?

- Where would you like things to go from here?

There are three parts to the Million-Dollar Question process. The first part (the mental part) of the process is to build the question. The second part is the delivery. As I said earlier, I like the idea of delivering questions, because in my mind it is similar to making an offer. It does not mean that the offer has to be accepted immediately in order to move the conversation forward. The third part, after you deliver a question, is to shut up, and listen!

Does my description of the third part sound harsh? Well, it is designed to get your attention—"shut up and listen!" gets right to the point.

If you can deliver a question and wait patiently for an answer, you will accomplish much more than you may realize. First, you allow your prospect to think about his or her answer before giving it to you. Waiting in silence dispels the perception that you might be more interested in selling something than connecting with the person you are speaking with.

- When someone listens intently to what you have to say, how does that make you feel?

- When someone cuts you off before you complete your sentence or your thought, how does *that* make you feel?

Remember Painful Selling Truth #1? "As soon as you start to sell, people can tell." Also remember that that's okay.

Asking Million-Dollar Questions immediately identifies you as someone who sells without being a jerk.

Your agenda is not the only agenda that matters. People buy based on emotion, and the emotions you want to evoke are comfort and trust. To achieve that you must be patient.

Think about this equation:

$$\text{Responsive} + \text{Reasonable} = \text{Control}$$

It means you can control a conversation without doing all or even most of the talking.

Recall another painful selling truth I cited: The more I listen to what you say, the more fascinating you find me. Sounds like common sense. But also recall what my late father said about that: "The problem with common sense is that it's not that common."

Whenever you express an interest in someone, it makes the conversation an *exchange*, as opposed to one-sided, and, thereby, more enjoyable for both parties. People who sell like jerks are not concerned with whether the people they sell to enjoy buying from them or not. Jerks are only interested in making all the money they can—respect, common sense, and common courtesy be damned!

Because you are reading this book, I think it's safe to assume you are not a jerk, or don't want to be one anymore, so let's move on to build great conversations, by formulating and delivering Million-Dollar Questions.

Format and Formula

As noted previously Million-Dollar Questions need to incorporate a do, a don't, and an emotional trigger. It is optional to add qualifiers and action verbs. In any case, you should add those after you feel comfortable building and delivering the basic questions, such as those listed here, which each contain an opening, a point of action, and an option:

- Question 1: How do you feel about that?
- Question 2: What do you think so far?
- Question 3: What do you like to see in vendors like us?
- Question 4: What do you hope to achieve this year?
- Question 5: What do you need to know about us, before it would make sense to get together face-to-face?

Note that question 5 is for professionals in commercial real estate, because that type of sale is so dependent on face-to-face meetings to begin a substantive conversation. It does apply to other industries, but it is one that the thousands of real estate brokers I have trained over the years love. It answers many questions for them, it prevents them from talking too much, and very often it nets them one of two end results:

- It gets them an appointment (they love that).
- It disqualifies the prospect, allowing the sales person to move on!

Here's a bonus Million-Dollar Question that adheres to the formula, but is a bit long. But sometimes it is worth going down that longer path, because it is a profoundly effective qualifier.

- How often may I call, so that I am not a pest, but don't miss an opportunity to help you?

Remember, Moving Conversations Forward is not about getting a deal today. It's about taking incremental, future-forward steps that continue the conversation. Multiple touches are required, especially if you sell something with a high price tag.

There is a lot of action in that last question. There is imagery, there is an emotional trigger, and it has a persuasive air. When you ask "How often . . . " as opposed to "Is it OK if . . . " you change the tone and tenor of the question, and you successfully avoid the yes/no trap.

Think about it this way: If you were to board a train, you would immediately sense the forward motion of the great steel machine. As you moved from the rear of the train to the locomotive, you would feel an even greater sense of forward motion. Similarly, when you are speaking to someone, imagine that conversation as taking place in a series of moving cars—as a train of thought. Each step in the conversation takes you into the next car/thought on the train. But what if you, without meaning to, ask a yes/no question, immediately transporting you and the person you are selling to one, two, or more cars back? You have to find a way to get to the front of the train again. What will you do? Have no fear, nonjerk salesperson, you can smoothly move one, two, or several cars forward at a time.

How? With Million-Dollar Questions, of course.

My Favorite Million-Dollar Question

"How's my timing?"

Now, it does not necessarily include an emotionl trigger, but one is implied. If timing is not good, people will

---

tell you, and that is very different from asking: "Is this an OK time to talk?" My version creates an invitation, while the other (Is this an OK time?) asks for permission.

Every person I have shared it with (especially those who were initially reluctant to use it) became believers once they tried it—and heard the answers it prompted. Look at its elegance and simplicity. It begs an answer; and because you are not a sales jerk, you know that just because you decided to call or meet with this person at this particular point in time does not predicate urgency or need on their part to buy from you.

When you ask this question, you are demonstrating (1) that you value the other person's time and (2) that you understand this may not be the ideal time for the prospect to make a decision.

I am a huge fan of patience. I say that now that both of my children have successfully grown into functioning, productive adults. My wife would be the first to point out that during their childhoods I did not exactly hold the patent on patience. But what parenting taught me over time was the value and beauty in exercising patience. By asking, "How's my timing?" you are demonstrating what is all too rare in people these days: patience and charity.

Try it a few times in the next few days. Try it with people to whom you may not be trying to sell anything. Try it, and follow through with the hard part: *Listen* for the answers.

John Travolta appeared in a movie entitled *Pulp Fiction* some years ago. One of the great lines from that film was delivered by Travolta's character: "Are you a person who listens, or do you just wait to talk?"

I was recently reminded of this quote by someone who told me that every time he thinks about that line, he feels as if someone is poking him in the chest. It is a question that prompts introspection. It is a call to arms! It is a profound and unsubtle reminder to resist our desire to speak, pontificate, and otherwise blab endlessly.

When I moved from New York to California, I had to join a support group for compulsive talkers, called On and On and On and On. Yes, I have been there. I have interrupted, and I have cut people off in midsentence. I have made horrific mistakes in front of influential people, and it is only now I can laugh at the difficulty of walking out of a meeting or presentation realizing that not only would I probably not sell anything to those people, but that I would remember that day for the rest of my life.

We all wish we could delete unpleasant memories from our minds the way we remove outdated files from computers. But, in truth, it is these unpleasant moments that teach us about ourselves—as well as give us a great resource of stories to share with others.

My good friend Dennis Napoliello runs sales throughout the United States for Equinox Fitness. He tells me that the best stories usually come out during his end-of-month road marathons. End-of-month can be fun for salespeople, but it is something of a nightmare for sales leaders. Salespeople will build up the hopes of the managers and VPs all month about the deals that "are a lock" (translation: "I hope to God this does come in, because I need it for quota!").

Leaders, managers, and VPs like Dennis take all of these promised windfalls with a grain of salt. Rather than call out these people, Dennis works with them, to bring in as much revenue at the end of the month as they can. As he runs around, working to help a particular rep close deals in a certain city, he might take his boss, or even one or two of the salespeople with him, to plan and strategize. This, Dennis says, is when the best stories emerge.

Start implementing (formulating and delivering) Million-Dollar Questions as soon as possible, regardless of where you are in the selling period as you read this. See if you can add two or three a day.

The key is to deliver the question (whether it is perfect or not is not the issue—just practice) and then wait for your answer. Let the person you are selling to THINK. Thinking will make them remember you, and it may very well gain you an invitation prior to your asking for it.

That is a wonderful experience that I hope you can create and re-create over and over in your selling life.

Remember that all things are possible if you remain open to the possibilities. If you view each conversation as a three-dimensional image, the opportunities and choices may appear limitless. Selling without being a jerk means that you keep your desire to close the deal today in abeyance, and your desire to serve and learn in the forefront of the conversation.

Million-Dollar Questions will serve you well, because they achieve multiple goals with minimal effort.

CONCLUSION

The expectations you bring to the selling conversation can be instrumental in the outcome you experience. Incremental, patient, forward-motion steps guarantee income down the road, and they also supply you with the necessary blocks with which to build a career.

Patience, process, thought, and listening—all of these are attributes of the person who sells without being a jerk.

With that in mind, I want to end this chapter with a few more examples of Million-Dollar Questions.

- What would need to happen before you would consider an alternative to your current provider?

- When it is time to choose a provider (or someone to represent you) what criteria will you use?

- What are the most important things I need to know about your business?

- How far in advance of your next budget planning session would it be appropriate for us to talk?

- How can I be a useful resource to you?

- How many people do you know that should go out and buy a copy of this wonderful little book RIGHT NOW?

Painfully True Selling Story # 6

I was making cold calls in the suburbs of Chicago. As a young, hungry, commission-only sales rep with three kids and a stay-at-home wife to provide for, I was determined to succeed. I had been fired from my previous sales job due to poor performance.

I was selling office supplies door-to-door in office complexes and industrial parks. One door that I ventured into proudly posted a "No Soliciting" sign (basically, a direct invitation for professional salespeople!). I was accustomed to opening every door, regardless of the ill-mannered suggestion that my profession could somehow be negated with a $2.50 window sign!

Opening the door, I encountered a well-poised, middle-aged woman. She looked me right in the eye and asked, "Did you see the sign?" I responded with "Huh, sign?" (something less than the honest truth) and waited for her comeback. She simply said, in a highly insistent tone, "Out! Get out!"

I withdrew from her front counter, which was just a few feet from the door. I opened the door and stepped just outside. Holding the door open, I turned her way and spoke firmly, "Can you hear me from here?" Her initially gruff exterior melted in an instant and she invited me back in. She became a "Top 5" account for me in no time, and we enjoyed that story many times in the years that followed.

That day, I learned that humor could not only open doors but also went a long way toward building relationships and closing deals.

—Rob Stubbs
Vice President of Sales
Express Personnel Services
Indianapolis, Indiana

CHAPTER SEVEN

HANDLING OBJECTIONS

E veryone starts somewhere. Early in my sales career, I worked in the greatest city in the world. For me, that means New York City. I have had the good fortune to travel far and wide in this wonderful world of ours, and though I may have been places more exotic (Singapore), more romantic (Paris), or prettier (San Francisco), as far as what cities should and do offer, New York is the greatest.

I make this rather biased statement because learning to sell in New York (and being able to make a living in the selling profession there) is a rare experience. Some cities may move as quickly, others may be tougher, but there is a bravado and sense of urgency, efficiency, and relevance in New York that cannot be found elsewhere.

Yet it fascinates me that some of the worst advice I ever got about selling I got in New York. Moreover, I have been given this advice over and over since; I have heard it repeated in sales training sessions and in sales meetings, and often quoted in movies and novels about the selling life. The advice is wrong, not to mention ludicrous, and most relevant to this book, it identifies where the line can be drawn between selling well and professionally and selling like a jerk. What's the advice?

Never take no for an answer.

What? You never want to take no for an answer? Does that mean that regardless of what people want, you are going to find a way to make them buy from you? If that's not a crime, at the very least it sounds like an unpleasant experience. Worse, it sounds like everyone giving this advice is promoting the idea that selling like a jerk is not only acceptable but *essential* to success in sales.

I did not choose sales; it chose me. I started in sales because I could not find a "regular" job. Most people who know me would never use the adjective "regular" to describe me, anyway, and that is fine with me. I am a drummer, husband, salesman, writer, comic, sales trainer, friend, father, and many other things, but *regular*? No way!

The selling life extended a hand of welcome to me after I had served four years in the U.S. Navy, where I had developed an appreciation for the results I could expect to enjoy as the fruits of my own hard work. The selling life and profession opened wide the doors of opportunity to me. Opportunity—with no limits.

Now, 23 years later, I have become evangelistic about what *is* appropriate, acceptable, and useful, and I have become an expert based on my experiences and observations on what is *not*.

As to the philosophy "never take no for an answer"; it flies in the face of everything I believe in. I love to sell. I love to close deals. I would like to stop typing this right now and go make a cold call. But I cannot, and never will, condone an approach or technique that makes people squirm. Never take no for an answer is the shortest distance between an opportunity to create an effective, long-term relationship and becoming truly annoying to your prospects.[1]

I find it amazing that an idea so flawed has been "sold" for so long, almost as the mantra of selling, and continues to persist in this profession. As a salesperson, you must be prepared for the fact that people will have numerous and myriad reasons for not buying.

One of your responsibilities as a salesperson is to listen to these responses, then weigh them to determine whether prospects are politely trying to get rid of you or are, in a sense, giving you an opportunity to learn more about how they make their buying decisions. When someone says, for example, "We never buy that sort of thing," or, "We don't see that as a fit for us," it may indicate that they are not able to make a decision or that they have decided at this time not to buy what you are selling. I say "may indicate" because, remember, we have to build a solid foundation for all relationships, and while these phrases may appear to be a threat to the structural integrity of a good relationship, they may also actually be *expressions of the truth.*

Now, take a minute to think about all the reasons that you, your marketing department, and your boss think that

---

[1]Remember, a prospect is different from a suspect or client.

you should sell more today than you did yesterday. Companies are in existence first and foremost to make a profit, and you have put yourself on the front lines of your company's relationship with those people who will determine the company's ability to generate profit. It's you against the buying world, and you have to accept the challenge, and you should (we hope!) want to do it without being a jerk.

HANDLING OBJECTIONS VERSUS OVERCOMING THEM

If you want to sell without being a jerk, then the distinction between handling an objection and overcoming one is a concept you will want to pursue, and its practice something you will want to master.

Here's what *handling* objections really means:

- It means that you have accepted the challenge of selling without being a jerk.

- It means that you want to pursue a different path from your peers and/or competitors.

- It means that you want to take a different approach from the traditional one, which is to behave as though objections are invitations to *sell harder*, or to pretend you don't hear the objections of your prospects.

Many salespeople have told me that they view objections as the prospect really saying: "You haven't sold me yet." I bristle at that interpretation (I have always wanted to use the word "bristle" in a book) because it teeters on the precipice of a dangerous selling vision and technique. Teetering on a precipice is *not* selling on a strong foundation. It does not leave you or the prospect with a positive feeling about the exchange.

This reminds me to remind you of Painful Selling Truth #4: *The salesperson who knows when to go away, lives to sell another day.* Being convinced that what you sell will help your prospect is not the same as *their* thinking it will help them. Further, even if they do believe that your product or service will change their life, their business, or their job for the better, that does not mean they will decide to buy that product or service from *you*.

The salesperson who recognizes, and points out, that the selling conversation might be better conducted either with another salesperson or another vendor opens the opportunity to be either:

- *Contradicted*: I have told people that I might not be the right provider for them only to have them refuse to let me off the phone. No one likes having their decisions made for them. (By the way, this is a great qualifying technique, as well.)

- *Thanked*: Yes, thanked! Do not let yourself hurtle down a tunnel full of conviction only to lose sight of the purpose of our profession. We want to sell, and we will sell, more reliably and more often in the long run *if* we know when to go away.

Being able to handle objections also demonstrates that you are a listener, ideally, a very good listener; and that single trait alone will set you apart from competitors.

So, if there is no way to avoid objections (and I have yet to find one), then what do we do with them? We certainly do not ignore them; nor do we try everything we can to dissuade someone from his or her current thinking. What we do is follow the "sell without being a jerk" blueprint, applying the design and construction rules I've described previously to this part of the conversation and to the ongoing formation of multiple and long-term relationships.

In short, now that you understand the fundamental tenets and thought processes of selling without being a jerk, it's time to prepare to take the steps that lead to the closing of a deal and the cementing of a relationship. In this chapter, that means addressing the four true objections.

THE FOUR TRUE OBJECTIONS

In all the years I have been selling, I have only been able to identify four true objections. That may sound surprising. It certainly seemed surprising to me when I first realized it. At the time, I held the position of sales trainer with the Vitamin Distribution Division of ICN Pharmaceuticals. While there I was tasked with writing a training manual, the first I was ever responsible for. When I got to the part addressing what salespeople should do when they encountered objections I had to come up with a specific process I wanted people to follow—think, act, measure response, adjust, respond, listen; think, act, measure response, and so on.

In the middle of writing about this, I became stumped over how to express the way I wanted the sales team to think about objections—what they mean and how to handle them. (I remember at the time being pleased with the epiphany I had to change the verb from "overcome" to "handle.")

As someone who loves to explain things in fine detail, I could immediately visualize how I would relate this information in my next training class. I also knew that no one was going to believe what I said just because I said it. But I was determined to truly influence and help the people I was training, partly (I admit) to feed my ego, but more importantly because the other part was the driving force behind me pursuing a job as a trainer—I had been selling for five years, had managed a sales team, and I was very clear in my own mind about what worked and what didn't. At that time, getting that information across was vital, because the bookstores across the country did not have a section dedicated to sales books, as they do now. Information about how to sell, and sell well, was hard to find. Sales was still a "try it—if you make it, great; if you don't, too bad" type of profession. Looking back, I would call it a pursuit rather than a profession. I am not even sure it was seen as a profession back then; maybe "pursuit" is a better word.

At that stage of my life (I had been married five short years and was the father of two young children), I had held a few different positions since exiting the Navy for the second time, and I had seen and heard traditionalist sales training, which from my point of view could be boiled down to these concrete steps:

1. Introduce
2. Uncover needs
3. Explain features and benefits

4. Conduct trial close

5. Overcome objections

6. Conduct trial close again

7. Use feel, felt, found

8. Conduct trial close a third time

This was an accepted, though less than exceptional, approach that had been in place for years, and the rationale behind continuing to use it was: "How could it be wrong?" To me, right or wrong was not the issue; rather it was finding the *best* way to sell. And that meant asking two important personal questions:

- How can I be a productive person of character?
- How can I go home at night and look my family in the eye, if I'm not proud of what I do every day?

I wanted to be as proud of *my* vocation as my wife (a nurse) was of hers. As I said, I had two young children at the time, and I knew they were listening at some level, while sitting at the dinner table or riding in the car, to what I said about the work I did. Aside from the sense of obligation I felt to be a good role model, even in those early years of my selling career I was also someone who enjoyed doing things well, whether playing an instrument, speaking in front of people, or being a friend, father, and husband. So, when I was charged with writing the training manual at ICN, I wanted it to be the best one my employer, the salespeople, and my wife had ever seen. And, of course, I wanted my sales team to think differently about what they were doing. If

I could offer them a unique way of thinking about the selling process (or if I could just get them to think about what they did *as a process*), then I would consider the manual a success.

So I walked the floor for a few days, thinking, while coaching and helping the sales staff turn orders for a few bottles of vitamins and mineral supplements into a full case of them ("We would be happy to pay the shipping!"). I whispered open-ended questions into the ears of the staff to encourage them to either wrap up the call or to advance their ordering process—"How does that sound?" "Which shipping option would you prefer?" And one of my all time favorites, "What else?"

As I walked around doing these things, I also *listened*. I listened to the salespeople talk to their neighbors after a call, and to how they debriefed the people around them. I listened to what they thought the reason or excuse or objection was that they could not "trial close" their way out of. I carried a notepad, writing down all of the alternatives I could think of to what I had heard. Later, when I reviewed my notes, I drew a line through any new words or phrases that had been used to express the same objections I had already noted. As a result of this process, the answer to how to handle—as opposed to overcome—objections became clear to me. And as a result of this process, I identified the four true objections. Here they are:

- No money
- No need
- No hurry
- No confidence

Take a few moments to look at these. Then we'll compare them to the most common ones you may have heard. I think you'll find that regardless of what reason someone gives you for not buying from you that reason or explanation will usually fit within one of the four categories.

This will be fun. OK, maybe not as fun as an amusement park ride, or a first class ticket to somewhere exotic, but if this isn't fun at some level, we shouldn't be doing it anyway. So, let's begin.

No Money

No money does not mean that a prospect's company cannot make payroll. It means that your call to the prospect may not be timely, or that the prospect does not think, feel, or believe that what you are selling will change his or her life or business *today*. As I've said before, that is okay. It really is. Your job is to Move Conversations Forward, qualify, and close. If you find that a company either does not have the budget for your product or service, or it just doesn't see why it should invest the amount of money you are asking for to acquire said product or service, then you must do one of two things:

- Plan a future conversation[2]
- Ask what would prompt the prospect to spend money on something similar to what you are offering.

---

[2]"OK, sounds like we should talk again. When might it be a good time for me to reach out to you in the future?"

I read a great book on sales some years ago entitled, *The One-Minute Salesperson*, by Spencer Johnson (Harper Collins, 1984). One point in particular resonated with me: the use of the phrase "your offer." Whenever you sell, you are making an offer. When you look at selling this way, it creates a mental picture that the interaction will be pleasant and fruitful for both the salesperson and the prospective buyer. It says I am not trying to force people to buy things; I am not trying to squeeze cash out of people. I am making an offer to those individuals and organizations that, based on my research, might have an interest in what I am offering.

And, as you make your offer, keep in mind that there is no obligation on anyone's part to buy from you. It is your responsibility to connect, be patient, encourage participative conversation, and then move that conversation forward.

This means that when someone says something that boils down to "No Money" (It's not in the budget, or it's too high-priced, or we can't afford something like that) what they are saying is:

- I do not see the value.
- We already allocated funds and spent that money elsewhere.
- It is not a priority on my list right now, so I can say anything, in order to get back to what I'm doing.

This is not the same as "they are lying to you." This is what I call "boiling down" their statement or response to a phrase that is something you can handle, as opposed to your feeling as though you need to "overcome" the objection and win every time. When someone gives you an objection, they are not trying to make you look foolish, nor are they trying to get rid of you. They are responding to what they have *heard*, not all of the knowledge in your head about how great your offer is. Take it, learn from it, see if you can find a way to continue the conversation.

I do not want you to "lie down" (give up) after the first objection. I just want you to be sensitive and realistic to what people are thinking, feeling, saying, and doing.

Handling Objections helps you to be a better professional, as do all of the caveats, ideas, admonitions, and instructions in this book.

No Need

"No need" does not mean that what you sell is not useful or valuable. It means that as the business day marches past the window of your prospects, they may have more important things on their minds besides your offer.

The no need objection is best dealt with by acknowledging that your choice to call or visit may not coincide with your prospects' need to purchase. One response I have heard multiple times in my selling life is, "We don't need that right now." Regardless of who is saying this, I have to accept what they say, yet find a way to move the conversation forward. In this regard, I want to offer you something that has worked for me many times. The first time I said this, it was a spontaneous remark, but it got the attention of my prospect, so

I tried it several more times, each time delivering it with less intensity, more warmth, and in a calmer tone.

> *"I can appreciate how miraculous it would be if on the specific day I called, you happened to have a need. My call today is intended strictly as an introduction, and to see if what I (we) do might be useful to you and your company* down the road."

This response to the no-need objection has netted me, and hundreds of my students, remarkable results. It breaks down barriers, and shows that I am considerate, that I have a perspective beyond today's call.

It also gives you one of my two favorite phrases to have ready to "drop into" a Million-Dollar Question. I am a huge fan of the phrases:

- Down the road

- In the future

Everyone you come into contact with will create a different mental picture of what period of time they choose to associate with those phrases. Here's a fun exercise: Ask three different people the same question: "What do you see happening down the road?"

Make mental note of the period of time they describe.

My son is a film editor. He has a unique perspective of time and deadlines. *Down the road* to him almost always means: "within the confines of the project I am working on" (translation: this week, or next).

My daughter, however, is a long-term planner, with many lists. *Down the road* (to her) could encompass the next five years of her life.

When you are dealing with the no need objection, you may have the prospect focused on the fact that they think that you want a buying decision from them today. Prevent that trap by asking what they plan, hope for, or are interested in achieving *down the road*.

> **Fun tip:**
> Try the same exercise, but replace "down the road" with "in the future." You will be fascinated (and potentially entertained) by the result. At the very least, you will learn something.

My point is that "No Need" need not be conversation killer. It may, prima facie, be the truth. You, as a salesperson who needs to make quota and pay your bills, may not be thrilled with this statement, but that doesn't negate its truth.

Each selling conversation comprises a wildly unpredictable set of potentialities. Thus, we have to follow a logical progression of thought, focusing on the issues. This means we cannot allow ourselves to be distracted. (See the 20 Call Burst in Chapter Five.) In simplest terms, the no-need response may actually mean that the prospect is not a qualified prospect. I'll say it again, "no need" need not be a conversation stopper; nor should it be a red flag to you that it is time to:

- Throw a list of features and benefits at the prospect's feet.

- Convince the prospect that he or she "just doesn't see the value yet."

- Prove to the prospect that his or her prior decisions were ill advised or uninformed.

Never forget, a primary goal of a sales call is to determine whether it makes sense to move forward. To do that, we have to commit to our selling intent and approach. And handling objections is the not the same as getting people to do what we want.

One more important point I want to make about the no-need objection: Don't take this response personally. It does not mean "never will need." It may simply mean: "That is not something that is a priority right now."

Timing is a challenging aspect in selling. You cannot determine in advance if your timing is good or not; it may be on the mark or fall just short, or even be way off. At the same time, keep in mind the old adage, "Chance favors the prepared mind," the lesson being that hard work—concentrated, focused, disciplined, measured, and patient hard work—will win out more often than not. So, when I call (or call on) more people than another salesperson, and I sell without being a jerk, I am constantly improving my ability (as well as my chances) to sell successfully. I prepare my mind, my sales desk, and my business, and that helps me to uncover more chances to sell, and to sell without being a jerk.

Your options in handling this objection are:

1) Plan a future conversation.
2) Find out what might be of interest to them, instead of trying to convince them that they need something—especially if they have already said: "No need."

Someone telling you that he or she does not need your product or service is not the end of the conversation. It is not a yes disguised as a no. It is only information, and we must take it at face value.

No Hurry

To handle this objection, the aforementioned issue of timing comes into play again. Instead of assuming the persona of a 1950s bag toter, I want you to build an inventory of emotional triggers to use with your targeted database or list of prospects. In the bag toter approach, in contrast, salespeople were assigned a neighborhood, and their job was to knock on every door in that neighborhood. Imagine the varied responses these guys would get! By the time the salesman had gotten to the end of his day, he would have been able to recite his pitch and presentation in his sleep. Modern-day selling (and by that I mean proper, professional, respectful selling—selling without being a jerk) dictates (or at least vehemently suggests) that you and I take a different approach, one particularly relevant to the No Hurry Objection.

If you engage people in conversations, *move the conversation forward*, and get invited to the next step of that conversation, you ensure that you will not lose a sale, because once you understand who your prospects are, what they like and how they buy, your selling job will become much easier. When you involve your prospects in the conversation, and refrain from selling through or by fear, they are going to be more inclined to speak to you once, twice, and many more times beyond that.

This is not to say that you will never hear the no-hurry objection, or that you will sell everything you want to sell every time you want to sell it. But you will become more familiar with the process of forming relationships with many people over a longer period of time.

Have you ever heard the saying: "I would rather have 10 percent of something than 100 percent of nothing?" I am not sure who said that, but it applies to several tenets of selling without being a jerk. For one, it says that if you accept selling a small order at the first opportunity, you open the door to sell more, rather than trying for too much too soon and ending up with nothing. If your goal is to first learn about the people to whom you want to sell, rather than focusing only on closing a sale, over time you will develop greater patience with the process. Patience, I think you'll find, can be almost as valuable as a cash-in-hand commission. It may not be something you can trade for goods and services, but think of it as an alternate investment, a deposit in the relationship account from which you can draw at some future date.

Reliable ways to handle the No Hurry Objection are:

- Plan a future conversation.
- Learn about their planning/buying cycle.

If the day you call is not the day for them to buy, throw the idea out that you would like to be considered before their next decision process. Great Million-Dollar Questions that will help you get this information, and yet not seem as though you are interrogating would be:

- How far in advance of the next evaluation period would it make sense for us to speak again?

- How would you like to have an alternative, when the time comes to review current providers?

- What time of the calendar year do you start sending out RFPs?[3]

I remind you once again of the importance of implementing the 20 Call Burst. By doing so, you will come to benefit from the aggregate power of that sort of patience, determination, and discipline. And you will come to hear more often these kinds of comments from your prospects:

"Funny you should call—I just walked out of a meeting where we were discussing that very issue!"

"Have you been talking to anyone else here?"

"I know that we have some concerns in that area. What prompted you to call today?"

All of these intimate that people are surprised and pleased when an enterprising, patient salesperson, *not a jerk*, calls at an opportune time, instead of when they are trying to get out of the office early to start a vacation, or attend a child's sporting event, or . . .

I have heard these exact sentences in my career. When they come, I have learned to take a deep breath, and to stay focused, patient, and professional, instead of "going in for the kill." People in general like to be pursued—which is entirely different from being "hunted down." Not selling

---

[3]Request for Proposal. This can be a necessary process to go through to earn business. If it is endemic in your industry, then get better at getting on RFP lists than anyone else. Don't try to circumvent the process. Doing an end-around on your prospect will only end in tears.

like a jerk means you don't perpetuate the age-old stereo-types about our profession, such as:

- All salespeople are pushy.

- Salespeople try to make customers spend more than they intend.

- Salespeople do not care about the people they sell to.

When prospects indicate they're in no hurry to make a commitment or decision, or do anything else that might net you a commission, regard it as an opportunity to discern when there might be an opportunity in the future. Ask one of the million-dollar questions I taught you: "How often may I reach out to you, so that I am not a pest yet I do not miss an opportunity to help you?" Keep in mind that your first meeting or call to a prospect is not the be-all and end-all of the opportunity. Quite the opposite! As long as you can obtain an invitation to return at a later date, to continue the conversation, you have achieved a reasonable goal.

No Confidence

When someone tells you they are not familiar with you or your company, or they indicate that they had tried a service like yours in the past with less-than-stellar results, they are telling you that they do not have high confidence in your offer. Be sure, as someone who sells without being a jerk, that you maintain the distinction in your mind between their not having confidence in your offer, and their not having confidence in *you*.

They do not know you. As a result, how could they trust you? This is where the cerebral part of the selling process comes into play. People buy based on emotion, and we have to control the conversation, without getting emotional about what we hear.

No confidence should not be a confidence shaker. There are a few different, and one or two intellectually challenging, ways to handle the no-confidence objection.

- Use feel, felt, found
- Get testimonials (verbal or written)
- Plan a future conversation

Feel, felt, found is old, and new. It is thoughtful and, I admit, a bit manipulative, in that it is probably the closest I will come to giving you a scripted response. It follows the tenets of not selling like a jerk, because if people do not want to hear convincing evidence to buy your product or service, they will not pull the no-confidence objection out of their hand of cards. When someone says something along the lines of, "We are not that familiar with your company," he or she is inviting you to educate them.

Feel, felt, found works like this:

"I certainly can appreciate how you *feel*, because one or two other folks have *felt* the same way, initially. Yet what they *found* was [insert an actual benefit here—e.g., "We actually saved them money." "We are reliable now that we have upgraded out technology."].

Then deliver this Million-Dollar Question:

"Based on that information, what would you like to do?"

Don't forget to end the response with a question, to follow the format and formula of selling without being a jerk. Be sure that you do not answer a question with a question, but make the conscious effort to follow each statement you make with a question!

TESTIMONIALS THAT SPEAK FOR YOU

Testimonials are wonderful, for a few reasons. First, they feel great to receive, because they are endorsements of the quality of work and service that you, the salesperson, provided. Even if your manager is attentive, and lets you know that they are pleased with your performance, it is not the same as having a satisfied customer take the time to say they are happy with you. Testimonials come in different forms, but my favorite is the letter on company letterhead.

When a client of mine has had a particularly satisfying experience with our company, I ask them: "How would you feel about writing a short note to us, printing it on your letterhead, and mailing it to me?"

Often (not all the time) but often enough, they agree. This fills my file cabinet with recently-dated hard copy letters that I can copy, or scan into a document and email to prospects who deliver the "No Confidence" objection.

When they read the testimonial that I send, they are not being pitched by me. They are being spoken to by a peer, and that has weight and might that your feature/benefit statements and genuine sincerity will never communicate.

Testimonials are powerful. If you ask people for them and they refuse, you may want to examine the quality of service you are providing. When you do win those testimonials, keep them handy, and ask: "How interested would you be in reading about another person's experience with our product/service/idea?"

If they agree, then off it goes, and you plan a time to continue the conversation. This does not remove the no confidence objection, but it is a solid and reliable way to handle it.

CONCLUSION

Learning to handle objections centers on one of the most important, and therefore often-repeated principles of selling without being a jerk: listening. It is about maintaining the 80/20 rule, and learning to respond, not react. Learning to handle objections means that just because you do not close a deal with Prospect A does not mean you will not close a deal with anyone.

Keep calling. Stay focused. Sell. Finally, remember that no matter how long you have been selling what you sell, or working where you work, if you lose your curiosity, you will lose your ability to learn.

Painfully True Selling Story #7

My business partner, Ken Apperson, and I have been selling together for many years. Before we became partners, we used to go out on calls together for a variety of reasons (safety in numbers; one of us would think of something to say or ask that the other didn't; etc.). This is the story of one funny call we made several years before we started Quagga.

We were trying to impress a prospect and convince her that doing business together would be very beneficial to both of our businesses. The decision maker was a young woman who seemed fairly new to the business world. We had been asking her questions about her responsibilities with the company, after which Ken made the seemingly innocent comment, "Wow, it seems like you wear a lot of hats around here!"

The prospect responded, "No, I don't really wear hats—they tend to cover my eyes."

At this point, my future business partner paused for a second. Then, this grown man started a giggle fit that was beyond his control, while I sat by horrified.

Finally, I attempted to perform damage control by saying, "No, it's just a saying . . . meaning you have a lot of different responsibilities with the company."

I seem to remember the meeting ending pretty quickly.

Needless to say, neither of us got a sale out of that meeting, but we did forge a lasting business partnership. And we still get a good belly-laugh over that story a few times a year.

—Scott Knorp
President
Quagga
Folsom, California

CHAPTER EIGHT

SELLING HONESTLY AND USING APPROPRIATE LANGUAGE

B ecause I love questions so much, I will begin this chapter with two that run on parallel lines of thought:

- How realistic do you think it is that your prospects have never been sold to before?

- Can you tell when someone is trying to sell you something?

Every time I hear a salesperson utter the phrase, "I am not trying to sell you anything" I cringe. Don't you? Think about it. What self-respecting person would take the time to call you, present an offer, and ask questions if he or she were not in the business of selling you something? Why participate in the charade? My answer: Because salespeople who do this are acting like jerks.

Herewith, more questions:

- Why do salespeople think that prospects have no idea that they are trying to sell them something?
- Why do most salespeople try to disguise their intent?
- Why do so many salespeople perpetuate the notion that one has to be a jerk to even work in sales?

Why have I asked you these without giving you any answers?

Because I want you to think, rethink, laugh, act, take a different perspective, and apply what you read here, so that you can *make more money*.

I want you to achieve this by committing to a standard of conduct and etiquette that will set you apart from every other salesperson calling on your prospects.

Selling without being a jerk means that you do not play "Wizard of Oz" during sales calls. What do I mean by that? No doubt you recall that Frank L. Baum's Wizard is a frightening character, but the fear he instills in people is based on trickery and distraction. The famous line when he is found behind the curtain working the noisemakers—"Pay no attention to the man behind the curtain!"—is similar in my mind to "I'm not trying to sell you anything": it's a not very successful distraction from the truth, from reality.

I don't want to sound unduly harsh here, however, as I acknowledge that telling someone you are not trying to sell them something is understandable, because often we salespeople get caught up in the moment and speak before we think. We've all had the experience of being shocked at what comes out of our mouths when we open them before we think through what we want to say. (See Phil Jakeway's Painfully True Selling Story #3 at the beginning of Chapter Four.)

I also want to acknowledge that salespeople often do not want, or intend, to sell like jerks. Rather, they do it as a defense mechanism, because they feel devoid of alternatives. Salespeople who miss the mark (and, I hope, as a result of your investment in this book, you will no longer be part of that group), and miss it over and over, tend to think, feel, or believe that the selling conversation is fundamentally different from all other conversations they participate in, and that the selling relationship is different from other relationships they are involved in.

In fact, conversations and relationships of whatever sort, in whatever arena, have a great deal in common. All people, not just salespeople, want to influence, convince, cajole, and "close deals." Think about it. Remember the last time you asked a friend or spouse, "So, what do *you* want to do tonight?" Didn't you already have a movie or restaurant in mind?

BEING UP FRONT ABOUT SELLING

To circle back to my point about knowing when you're being sold to: Simply put, if you can tell when someone is trying to sell you something, of course your prospects can tell when you're doing it, too. It follows then that your sense about this experience is based on the fact that someone has sold to you before. Maybe it was a coach who tried to convince you that you should be playing a different position than the one you coveted so fiercely when you showed up for the team's first practice. Maybe it was the guys in your neighborhood who tried to coerce you into staying out later than your curfew. Maybe your best friend talked you into cutting (ditching) school for the day. Whatever it was, someone early in life successfully "sold" you an idea, a choice, or a process. So, let's be honest; let's agree to enter sales conversations knowing that two dynamics are already in play.

- People can tell when you are selling something.
- They have been sold to before.

Where does that leave us, as salespeople?

As you might imagine, I have some ideas about how to answer that last question. In Chapter Seven, I made the clear distinction between *overcoming* objections and *handling* them, pointing out how a single word can effect significant change in your attitude and approach to this very challenging aspect of the selling process. I want to continue with that approach in this discussion about people knowing that you are trying to sell them something.

Yvette Koebke is one of he funniest, smartest, and most accomplished professional salespeople I have ever met. She has been selling in the hospitality industry for a many years. We met when we were both instructors at a corporate university experience in Arizona. She said something during the introduction to her speech that I've never forgotten, and it bears repeating here: "As soon as you tell them who you are, and where you are from—the secret is out! They know you are a salesperson!"

RECOGNIZING THE POWER OF WORDS

Once the secret is out, what do we do about it? We have to take a proactive and direct, yet reasonable and patient, tack to engaging prospects in selling conversations so that we sell to them without being a jerk. To that end, I have carefully devised five Million-Dollar Questions for you to adopt and adapt to your offer, with a twofold purpose in this context: to unveil the selling "wizard" and to help you Move Conversations Forward. Try one or more of them, and let me know which have been effective for you (or, if you prefer, you could just send me a portion of your next commission check—a single-digit percentage is sufficient). These questions are constructed to enable you to determine what your prospect thinks of your offer.

- How does this compare to other [products, services, ideas] you have looked at?

- What are the three key things you are looking for in a [product, service, offer] like ours?

- How do you see a [product, service, idea] like this being of use in your organization?

- How can we best determine whether this [product, service, idea] will be useful to your [team, people, folks, organization]?

- How far down the road do you see yourself choosing a [provider, supplier, vendor] for this [product, service, idea]?

The words in brackets are options, for you to choose from as appropriate. Notice I did not use words such as "solution," "fix," or others that make bold, Wizard-like promises. Such words irk me, rub me the wrong way. They may not bother you, and that's fine. My point here is that you consider the power of the words you choose to sell your product, service, or idea. Recognize the effect they will have on your prospects and if you're failing to sell successfully, consider the alternatives—another way of saying something, selling something.

I told you about my first corporate sales training position with ICN Pharmaceuticals. In that role, I conducted classes and conducted one-on-one coaching with the salespeople. During one particularly busy day, I was encountering a fair amount of resistance to some practiced and planned questions I had developed for the team. Who knows why—maybe there was a weird convergence of the stars—but whatever the reason or cause, I was getting stonewalled at every turn. Finally, one of the recalcitrant reps said to me: "Klymsh, I don't have any alternatives!"

To which I replied, "There are *always* alternatives!"

That immediately sparked debate, conversation, as well as an outpouring of creative energy among the salespeople in attendance.

"What if we say this, instead of that?"

"Why don't we open the call a different way?"

"What can we ask them that will get them talking to us?"

These questions and others like them turned the day around as the sales team came to realize the truth in my refrain that there are always alternatives. It's something you need to keep in mind for yourself as you go about learning how to sell without being a jerk. Don't box yourself in. Don't think that this particular list of prospects is going to be the nirvana of all cold calling. Don't assume that a question that worked with LMN Company will work with OPQ Company.

When you approach selling with the belief that there are always alternatives to everything you do, when you remind yourself you have options, you'll find the door to the creative universe to be wide open, all day, every day. And nowhere is the idea of taking advantage of alternatives more powerful than in the language you use to sell to your prospects. Language alone can make the difference between selling like a jerk and selling like a consummate professional.

Of course, you'll have to experiment. And, of course, that means you'll make mistakes. But it's your willingness to make mistakes that's key to finding the alternatives that work for you. Earlier in the book, I mentioned my assistant, Taryn. When she came to work for me, she had limited experience in a business environment. Nevertheless, in her previous jobs as a lifeguard and pool manager, she had learned to manage, and had performed exceptionally. But she wanted to learn about business, as it had been her major in school. To help her do that, I told her I wanted her to do three things every day.

- Ask a lot of questions.
- Try something new.
- Make mistakes.

These three instructions add up to Painful Selling Truth #2, which I introduced in Chapter Two: "Experience may not be the most patient teacher but it's the most effective."

Learning to Speak to Your Prospects

Regardless of the way people talk in your office, department, or company regarding your product, service, or idea, the language we use with prospects, suspects, and clients has to be familiar to *them*, comfortable for *them*. That is, you must remove all company- or product-/service-specific lingo. This is not always easy to do, as the way we talk to our colleagues becomes second nature, so we tend to continue in that vein with our prospects. Thus, it's imperative that you remain attentive to your "audience."

Similarly, be on the alert against talking over someone's head. This, too, you may do unintentionally. You're so familiar with your product or service that you forget your prospects are not. Or you fall into the habit of trying to impress them with your knowledge, believing that will convince them to buy from you. More often than not, however, it annoys people and so it has the opposite effect.

My son works for a major television network as an assistant film editor. He is skilled in using editing software, digitizing tools, and all sorts of other technical devices, tools, and toys. I recall when he graduated from an editing workshop, and he and I were having dinner to celebrate. He seemed to be speaking a new language entirely as he described his experience. I beamed with pride as he explained to me about transposition, fade-ins, and drag-and-drop editing, but I was also aware he assumed I knew what he was talking about. (I didn't have a clue!) Salespeople make the same mistake. So always remember to adjust your vocabulary when you explain your product or service, and ask questions to ensure you've been understood as you intended.

Learning to Understand Your Prospects

At the same time we salespeople must adjust our language to suit our prospects, we must also learn to speak and understand the language of their businesses—they are, after all, the "customer."

For example, I do a fair amount of work with people in the commercial real estate world (brokers, developers, leasing professionals, real estate investment trusts, etc.). When I first started selling to them, I felt bombarded by the various acronyms, lingo, and shorthand they spoke in. I felt lost. But because I was selling to them, I had to learn *their* language—not with the objective of being able to talk like an insider, but so that they would be able to speak to me comfortably and easily.

To learn to speak your prospects' language, I again recommend you listen more than you speak and formulate and ask topic-appropriate Million-Dollar Questions. In this way, both parties continue to become more comfortable over time; and you earn their trust and demonstrate you are interested in developing a long-term relationship with them.

The important point here is, speaking your prospects' "internal" language will get *them* talking, which is what you want; it's how you move conversations successfully forward. Salespeople are perceived as jerks when they do not take the time to learn about their prospects before they start selling—ideas, features, benefits, and so forth.

Warning

Learning to speak your prospects' language is guarding against making assumptions about your prospects' organization or buying history, especially if you have never done business with them before. The price for doing this is high.

Learning to Listen to Your Prospects

Yes, I've talked about the importance of listening more than speaking during selling conversations. But it bears repeating in the context of monitoring the salesperson's tendency to *push* our product, service or idea. We used to call the overwhelming urge to tell a prospect every detail of our offer "feature puking." Not a pleasant image, I know, but I think you know what I mean. The best position to be in when someone is feature puking is on the buying end. As a purchasing agent or buying decision maker at any level, this automatically puts you in a powerful negotiating position. Why? Because people who do this often sell like jerks, because they feel that as long as they are talking, they are controlling the conversation. Yet we know nothing could be further from the truth. Here's another adage I recommend you put in your memory bank: "I have never learned a single thing while I was talking!" How can anyone possibly learn anything while running their mouths? When I was in boot camp at the beginning of my Navy career, the company commander used to deride us for "jacking our jaws." I remember that phrase 30 years later, and it still serves to remind me not to talk when I should be listening, for when I forget, I inevitably miss important information, the same way we recruits missed the simple instructions the commander had just given everyone in the company.

CONCLUSION

Using language that your prospects can understand is one of the primary signs of a great communicator. My definition of communication is, "The positive, progressive, exchange of ideas." So, to communicate in the selling environment, you have to resist the temptation to tell others what to do, or try to direct outcomes. Make your prospects comfortable enough with you that they tell you what *they* think, like, want, and enjoy.

When I start a selling conversation, and ask a question or two or three, I tend to have unique and satisfying experiences. Prospects tell me what a great idea it was that I called them that day. Truly! Sometimes they even convince themselves it was such a good idea they must have thought of it themselves.

And remember, of course your prospects have bought before. That means you'll have to earn their respect, and the right to be the one to sell to them *this* time. Selling, as you well know, is not for everyone. But if you decide to accept the challenge I put forth in this book, to learn to sell without being jerk, it can be for you. Prior to being exiled, Napoleon Bonaparte said "France has more need of me than I of her." Not so for those of us in sales: The profession does not need us.

By virtue of the fact that you're reading this book, I assume you have decided that you love this profession and want to be one of those salespeople who is forthright and honest, and wants to sell, and sell a lot, without being a jerk. So, onward!

Painfully True Selling Story #8

For the past 15 years, I have been selling hotel room nights and meeting space. One day early in my career, I was cold-calling and was lucky enough to get in front of a decision maker. We immediately hit it off, because we found we had a lot in common—golf, travel to the Virgin Islands, and a love of a few Italian restaurants in town. So, I very quickly developed a rapport with this woman, and we were soon talking as if we'd been friends our entire lives.

At one point, I asked her which hotel she was currently using for her out-of-town visitors, and she replied, "We always use the Holiday Inn."

I quickly retorted (and this is an accurate quote), "Oh that hotel sucks. It's dirty and hasn't been renovated in years. Why on earth would you use that property?"

She snarled back, "Because my mom is the general manager there."

I could not get out of there fast enough!

> —Toni Jacaruso
> VP of Sales
> Dimension Development
> Arlington, Texas

CHAPTER NINE

CLOSED SALES AND CLOSING SALES

I am the kind of person who generally needs a few powerful, attention-getting experiences before I learn life's lessons. An example is a set of experiences that taught me the definition of a *closed deal*.

But before I share those stories with you, I feel compelled to first address the whole concept of *closing*.

CLOSING: KEEPING YOUR EYE ON THE PRIZE

Definitions aside, closing is something of a mystical experience, in that it can happen without you knowing it and, conversely, can slip away just as mysteriously. In terms of the latter, when you are busy selling, you have to remain attentive, or there is a very good chance you'll miss the close and, essentially, sell yourself right out of an order.

Listening to or watching a salesperson sell *right through* the close is similar to watching your child learn how to ride a bike. You know they both have to fall, and fall hard, but by doing so they'll eventually learn how to keep their balance. As in life, balance is difficult to achieve in the selling profession. And when you consider the 80/20 rule, which I mentioned earlier in the book, you can't help but observe that the concept hardly speaks of balance. But that formula, like every other idea, recommendation, and exhortation in this book, is what makes the selling profession so challenging, and why so few succeed in it. You must fail in order to understand, appreciate, and experience success. You have to blow a few opportunities before you develop an eye and ear for how to take advantage of them.

Throughout the book, you've been reading the painfully true selling stories of others in this field. In this chapter, I share one of my own, as it speaks about what closing a deal means. It exemplifies how important patience and process are to selling, and how making assumptions can get us into uncharted, dangerous territory.

My Most Painful—and True—Selling Story

One of the first rules of prudent money management is to pay yourself first. Another is that you cannot spend money you do not have. Well, thanks to credit cards, you and I know that the second rule does not really apply so much anymore.

To a salesperson, *sales projection reports* are a lot like credit cards, though they differ in a few ways. (Your company may have a different name for these reports, perhaps "budget" or "goal," but I think "sales projection report" is a more accurate term—for example, your personal money manage-ment budget is a lot different from your assigned sales bud-get.) The most prevalent difference is that when you use a credit card you are told when to stop—you have an as-signed limit. Sales projections, in contrast, are always more fluid, because salespeople either project lower than they think they will actually achieve, and hope for recognition for going over a low number (if you figure that out, please call me!); or they are told what their budget is, and they stress out all day, and most nights, about how far they are from achieving it.

The fact that I have worked on a sales team does not qual-ify me to comment, criticize, or instruct anyone in the pro-fession. However, the fact that I have worked on, managed, and sold as part of teams in several different industries over a 23-year career does qualify me to comment and instruct, because over that period of time, I have witnessed those ideas and practices that are transferable. Thus, I am not say-ing that the Million-Dollar Questions I outlined in Chapter Six are the only sales questions that work, only that, of the ones I have heard over the years in various industries, they got the best response. Furthermore, I believe that in order to Move Conversations Forward in the manner and with the intent I've been describing, Million-Dollar Questions and the 20 Call Burst are the best ways to facilitate that selling experience.

With a reinforcement of the ideas I've presented in mind, allow me now to take you to a place every salesperson I have ever worked with has been. And, of course, the best way to demonstrate to you that I know what this experience is like is to describe how I went through it. Remember, "experience may not be the most patient teacher."

When I was an executive recruiter, I was struggling to close my first deal. Specifically, I was having a very hard time adjusting to the velocity of deals among the executive ranks because I had spent the previous four years placing people in administrative and clerical jobs, positions that were fun to fill because it was a fast-moving, quick turnaround type of sale. I would send three or four people out on an interview with a potential employer, and the hit rate was pretty high—I (or one of my colleagues) would make a placement almost daily. Then I got the bright idea to "move up" to executive search, where things moved much *slooooooower*.

I was getting nervous. I was on a *draw*, and I wanted to start seeing some commissions come in to "cure" that draw. (For those of you who have never been "on a draw," it's essentially a loan from your employer. Each time you earn a commission, the first place that money goes is to pay back ["cure"] that draw. Obviously, the goal is always to get off draw, ASAP.)

Just as I was beginning to regret my decision to move up to executive placement, something wonderful happened—or so I thought: I had three different people go out on interviews to the same company in the same week. (Compare this to two to four people out on interviews *per day* in admin/clerical placement, and you understand the difference in activity.) Moreover, these three people were being interviewed by the same person at that company, so I thought I might have a chance at closing a deal. And after I spoke with the interviewer following the third interview, I learned he was very pleased with the people I had sent, so I thought my chances were even better.

"So, what happens next?" I asked him. (Sounds like a Million-Dollar Question, doesn't it?)

"Well, I will think about this over the weekend and let you know my decision Monday," he replied.

Needless to say, my imagination went into salesperson overdrive. If asked what could possibly have happened next regarding my pending sale, I would have given you 10,000 different scenarios.

By now, dear reader, you are probably a step ahead of me, since I have been foreshadowing the end result. But not so fast, as it gets much more interesting than you might think.

I was feeling cautiously optimistic for the remainder of that day. I avoided discussing the state of the deal with any of my coworkers. I even refrained from telling my wife anything about this particular selling conversation, because I knew she was hoping I would close something soon. So was my manager. So was I.

As I drove home that night, I replayed the conversation I had had with the decision maker earlier that day. (What else could I do?) I thought about his intonation, his pace, his demeanor, even his necktie. (Although we had talked only over the phone, I became so involved in thinking about, dissecting, replaying, and cogitating about this one deal that had the potential to change my selling month I actually found myself wondering what color tie the man was wearing!)

I made small talk with my beautiful wife that evening, not giving into the urge to share any details of my selling day with her. I went to bed, and woke the next morning having made a decision: that I was going to win this deal! I had come to the conclusion that all of my experience and knowledge pointed to the closing of the transaction, followed by the issuance of a commission check large enough to cure my draw. So sure was I that I drove to a travel agent's office and purchased a cruise vacation for my wife and me.

Shocked?

I'm not surprised.

When I went to work Monday, as soon as it seemed reasonable, I called the hiring authority at the aforementioned company, who promptly told me that he had indeed made a decision over the weekend: that his *internal* candidate was better suited to the position than anyone I had sent him. Moreover, he had already called this person Sunday, to ask if he would be interested in the promotion. The person accepted! That meant I had already spent money I now owed to someone else.

I was so focused on what I hoped *would* happen that I lost sight of what *could* happen. I had taken draw money and spent it under the assumption that I had already earned it.

Selling, as I've said so often, is a delicate razor's-edge balancing act. You must sell without being a jerk. You must openly admit to your prospects that you are trying to sell, and you must make them feel it is a good idea to continue the conversation.

Oh! And one more, minor thing: you have to understand Painful Selling Truth #5:

The appropriate time to celebrate the sale is *after* the commission check clears your bank.

I thought I had learned this lesson a few years earlier, when I was in the clerical placement business. In that business, the placement company offers employers who hired its candidates a 30-day guarantee, within which time they can have their money back. With "contingency" fees, the employer has time to determine whether the candidate recommended by the placement company is going to work out.

- If the person referred was offered a job, started on the agreed date, and lasted 31 days, then our fee was due and payable.
- If the person left or was asked to leave? No fee.
- If (and this is where a sense of humor in sales really pays off) the employer received our invoice and paid it before the 30-day guarantee had expired, I, the salesperson, would receive a commission.

Cool, right?

Unless you have the hideous experience called a *fall-off*.

If you are paid, and the employee does not work out, *you* have to pay *back* the commission out of future checks!

Not so cool.

Experience may not be the most patient teacher. . .

I thought I had learned my lesson not to spend my commissions until I had earned them, but apparently, as I mentioned at the beginning of this chapter, I need to learn my lessons several times before they stick.

I had booked a vacation with money that I had not earned yet. Now, the ensuing conversation I had to have with my wife was . . . well, let's just say, it was not fun. You can imagine.

GETTING EMOTIONAL

Emotional control is, I believe, a fantasy. I don't think we can control our emotions. This is not to say, however, we can't control how we respond to, react to, or deal with them.

The most consistently regular producers in the selling profession I have known and worked with have been highly emotional people. And, I hasten to add, over 70 percent of all CEOs of Fortune 500 companies have come from, or spent considerable time in, the sales ranks. Sales is not only the world's second-oldest profession, it is an honorable one and an excellent training and proving ground.

Sales, as I pointed out in Chapter One, is the engine of any capitalist economy. Sales put the clothes on your back, the car in your driveway, the movie you are planning on renting next . . .

Selling without being a jerk is knowing how to make people feel good about making a positive decision to move the selling conversation forward with me (or you), today.

With so much riding on the selling experience, how can you or I *not* get emotionally involved in sales conversations? However, you can feel certain emotions during the sales conversation or during the selling process without letting them be the driving force behind your technique. Keep in mind, the more emotionally involved you become, the less control you have.

What I have learned via the pain of experience, and am sharing with you in this book, is to treat every sales conversation as if it were part of a process. We either must work our way through processes to a conclusion, or we become mired in them. Life is not like a Hollywood movie. There are very few real-life story lines that neatly wrap up inside of two hours.

There are always alternatives, but not if you're focused on the past. Never forget: looking over your shoulder means taking your eyes off the road. Once a potential sale or deal is lost, it is important that you learn from the experience and quickly move on to the next. When you continue to dwell on a deal or conversation that did not come to the conclusion you had hoped for, you prevent yourself from working through the process. When, instead, you learn from your mistakes, ask a lot of questions, and try something new on a regular basis, you keep your mind open, your heart full of hope, and your future looking bright.

VISION PRECEDES EVERYTHING

"Vision precedes everything," is the opening statement in my book *The Ultimate Sales Managers' Guide*. I repeat it here because in the same way that your employer, executive, or direct manager must have a vision for the team, you must have a vision of your individual life in sales. But before you can make any visionary plans, you must have enthusiasm for the journey, the battle, and the process.

Enthusiasm for the process is absolutely imperative to have, because it gives you the energy to take stock every so often, and examine how you might improve. It also helps you to view things with a sense of wonder, which will help you ride out the very intense sales storm called quota.

No one is responsible for your income but you. You know that. So you have to find some balance between where you are now and where you want to be. For that you need a vision; without it, you will be stuck living day to day, hand to mouth.

Part of having a vision is recognizing you cannot control what is going on in the life of those you call on. So let those short, curt, or even rude responses roll off your back. When someone turns you down, do not take it personally. He or she is rejecting your *offer*. Your offer is separate and distinct from you.

In football, coaches tell quarterbacks they must have a short memory for bad plays. When an interception is thrown, or the receiver runs an incorrect route and the quarterback nets an interception, the quarterback is advised to learn from the error, regardless of who is involved or to blame.

Another aspect of vision, I believe, is to love learning. I think that is what drives me to cold-call after 23 years of making a living at it. Yes, money is a motivator for me, but I sell because it is endlessly fascinating and constantly challenging. And one more thing: Not everyone can do it well, over a long period of time, and I'm proud to be one of those who can. I have seen people come and go in the selling profession, and many are motivated by the future—they want to be able to say: "Oh, I did sales for a while," before they move on to something else. I say I'm in the selling profession because I love it.

In the next, and last, chapter, I will bring the ideas, concepts, techniques, and admonitions I've presented so far together in a useful, inspirational way.

It's Only Funny if It Applies to You

Each of the eight Painfully True Selling Stories in this book has a dual purpose: to make you laugh and to demonstrate a point.

One of the best teachers I ever had made me laugh, and often. As a result, I could not wait to hear what she had to say next, regardless of whether she was discussing American history or the latest adventures of her eight-year-old son. She brought a truth to each lesson and a genuine human element to everything she did. I remember her class because all the students were always on time, and most of us had actually completed a good portion of our homework. What made me laugh the most were the stories she told that hit a personal chord with me. When I tell someone a Painful Selling Truth, many times people will laugh. My response to (and gratitude for) their laughter is best summed up in the statement:

"It's only funny if it applies to you!"

This book is about you, me, and everyone else who has the courage to try to make a living as a salesperson. I want you never to forget that selling is a human activity, fraught with opportunity for error, and that making errors does not make us jerks—just members in good standing of this funny, unpredictable, and very curious human race.

Professional selling is a diverse community, one spread across all disciplines and industries. Yet there are many things that all professional salespeople have in common. One of the most important is a desire to connect with others.

In addition to sharing with you the lessons I've learned during my sales career, I am also interested in learning from you. So I ask you to submit your Painfully True Selling Story for inclusion on my blog or Web site. Please email your story to coachk@generatorinc.com. And don't hesitate to also submit questions, book feedback, even restaurant recommendations! I look forward to hearing from you!

Now, keep reading to find out how to ultimately tie all this wisdom together.

—John Klymshyn

CHAPTER TEN

BRINGING IT ALL TOGETHER

B y now, you no doubt have a sense of how fascinated I am with language. It is this fascination that will set the structure for the remainder of *How to Sell without Being a JERK!*, for I want language, and the way you use, respond to, and deal with it to be in the forefront of your mind as you commit to selling without being a jerk.

In the Foreword, Joe Harbert noted that we all sell—to our siblings, coworkers, families, and friends. How we sell is, like most things involving relationships, about choices. An important choice I made early in my selling career was to never participate in the "bait and switch" style of selling. This is when a certain item is advertised with the express purpose of bringing in the largest cross section of potential customers. The featured item is typically a "one at this price" offering, geared to get the buying public excited, and thus careless about reading the fine print. Bait and switch has been a selling technique for as far back in history as I have been able to discern. But it really is no technique at all; bait and switch is, simply, a gag, a trick, a deception.

In contrast, I determined this book would be about what I have found to be true, and truly useful, practical, and applicable techniques for those of you in the sales profession who want to sell without being a jerk.

EIGHT WORDS THAT BRING IT ALL TOGETHER

Now I will do what I always hope instructional books will do: bring it all together—the concepts, ideas, and feelings I have developed during my career in the world's second oldest profession.

Enthusiasm

Enthusiasm is essential if you want to be able to sell without being a jerk. Enthusiasm can give you the impetus you need to prepare yourself for a 20 Call Burst, and it can help you to maintain the focus required to get through that very necessary, very difficult, yet very productive activity. Enthusiasm can also help you to hold on until Friday, should that be the kind of week you're having—and we all have them. Sometimes, enthusiasm is all you can count on to get you to the next step.

Many people feel that enthusiasm comes entirely from within. There are industries built on motivational training concepts that insist that everything you do, or are capable of doing, must come from inside you. My view is somewhat different. Specifically, I don't believe any of us should put all the pressure on ourselves to be the sole font of enthusiasm.

I admit to needing help; in particular, I admit proudly that a small group of close friends, confidants, and advisors have gotten me through more than my share of difficult times in my career. To me, enthusiasm comes from sharing, and shared, experiences. Enthusiasm can be contagious, it can be nonexistent, it can be in great supply or mysteriously absent. Even when you want something, that does not mean you automatically have the enthusiasm to pursue it.

Salespeople across the world have one thing in common: desire. Desire is not the same as enthusiasm. Desire can dissipate when there are setbacks. Enthusiasm fuels our desire; it is fuel for the energy engine inside each of us. Fuel is not manufactured by the engine; it comes from other sources. My point: Do not dissipate your energy trying to be the only source of enthusiasm for yourself. Seek out others who do what you do, even if they are not selling the same thing you are. Join networking groups, business breakfast groups, or similar associations. There are many of these in every locale. Attend one or two of their meetings until you find one suitable to you, where there are others who face similar challenges to those in your daily selling life. And don't forget to look for fun! Find a group or groups where the members share a sense of humor and want to have fun doing what they do.

Focus

"Hocus pocus, I gotta stay focused!" As a manager, I truly wanted the people I trained and supervised to do well, so over the course of my eight-year management career, I had employees chant this phrase periodically. I still quote it to people who are struggling with start-and-stop-and-don't-finish-tasks syndrome. Read that statement aloud a few times (however silly it may appear) and see if it does not stay in your head for a while. Like the repetition and verbal practice required to learn a foreign language, I have found that saying this phrase repeatedly is an effective technique to remind myself to focus on whatever task is at hand.

My wife and I are planning trips to both Montreal and Paris in the next few months, so I am currently "brushing up" on my French. (OK, brushing up makes it sound as if I am already fluent in French. I have been to France *once*, seven years ago, and struggled mightily with the cadence and tempo of the native speakers.) I am listening to a language course, and repeating what they say, so that I am not self-conscious about pronunciation when I visit those two French-speaking cities.

For fun, I am also typing some ridiculous sentences into a translation program, because I would like to see the look on someone's face when I ask: "Where is the bakery that smells like feet?" or "How long will it take to paint this shoe?" My wife, of course, would never encourage this sort of silly behavior, so she will not know I am even planning it until she reads this book (which will be after we return!).

Look at that! I lost focus! And you were happy to come with me! Focus is a difficult issue for salespeople (all of us salespeople!), because we have so many interests, and so many items and ideas we need to tend to. The only way to make sure that all you have read in this book makes any impact beyond the printed page, is to find a way to maintain your focus as a salesperson.

Focus means that you can handle distractions, that you do not allow them to reprioritize your day. I suggest you assign a specific weight of importance to your daily tasks by putting them into the following three categories. The goal is to evaluate them based on a measure of their relative importance throughout your business day:

- Necessary
- Immediate
- Urgent

The items you identify as urgent must be tended to and completed before anything else. Those that are immediate must be completed before you leave your workplace for the day. And those you mark as necessary you can do over time, as long as you meet their deadlines, to ensure they never make it onto your immediate or urgent lists.

If you need help, ask someone to hold you accountable to regular cold-calling. If you need help developing the habit of staying focused, ask a friend who does not sell for a living to call you every so often, and ask one question: "When did you do your last 20 Call Burst?" That will be your signal to drop everything, and set up a 20 Call Burst for tomorrow, or this afternoon!

In summary, being focused ensures that you are doing the *right* thing at the *right* time for the *right* reasons.

Discipline

"Discipline" is derived from the word "disciple," my definition of which is, "One who is following a regular, proven path." Note that my definition does not address whether you are thinking about or planning to follow that path. It is stated in the present tense—the *now*, that fleeting, irretrievable moment. It is something you may prepare for (for quite some time), yet it is gone in an instant. An awareness of *now* creates the sense of urgency you need to stay focused.

Developing and maintaining discipline is difficult, yet *becoming* disciplined yields regular, and increasingly satisfying results. I know, because the discipline I learned as a musician (four beats to the measure, stay in time, wait your turn to play, practice in order to perform well) has stayed with me my entire life. Learned, practiced, self-denying discipline carried over to many aspects of life, and it was reinforced during my service in the U.S. Navy: *Do what is expected of you, in the best possible way that you can, show up on time, know your assignment, and see it through to its effective and accurate conclusion. Show respect for your superiors, and honor the chain of command.* These are solid, society-building tenets and constructs.

Discipline is, to some degree, about sacrifice, but the results can be immensely gratifying, and will pay dividends at near cosmic levels. What are you willing to sacrifice to make more money this year than you did last year? If it takes you a while to answer that question, you may need to examine how truly disciplined you are. Don't misunderstand me: Discipline is not punishment. It is about holding yourself accountable to expectations, the expectations of others, as well as those you have of yourself. There is an ancient book that says, "Discipline is necessary for instruction." In all of my coaching and teaching experience, I can attest to the fact that the people who learn the most are the ones who are willing to be taught. Wherever you are in your selling life, become disciplined. Today.

Listen

You have two ears and one mouth for a reason. This reminds me of the time I spoke in front of an association of hospitality accountants in Los Angeles about 15 years ago. I said that we should listen 80 percent of the time, and respond 20 percent of the time, "which is why we have two ears and one mouth!" I confidently added. At the first break, three of the association members approached me, and one of them said, "You realize that your percentage breakdown is off, right?" I must have responded with a blank look, because he elaborated: "It's actually 66 and 33." The trio found this quite amusing, and I later used it to good effect with the rest of the attendees.

Listening, as far as I am concerned, is the most underrated yet most essential skill you must develop to sell without being a jerk. Everything I teach, espouse, endorse, and prescribe is centered on the importance of listening. Listening is NOT waiting for the other person to stop talking so that you can begin. Nor is listening waiting until the other person says something you can use to convince him or her that he or she should buy from you. Rather, listening is an active, disciplined activity that requires you to stay focused.

I encourage salespeople to conduct selling conversations (Move Conversations Forward) by following a logical progression of thought (i.e., your calling today does not mean the prospect is ready to buy), with a laser focus on the issues (the last eight words that anyone says carry the emotional impact of their message). Listening is where selling without being a jerk begins and ends. It is the easiest thing to learn but the hardest thing to practice. It is the one guaranteed approach to conversations that will help you to connect with people of any race or gender, any education, any attitude, any level of income, any time, anywhere, under any circumstances.

Everyone is convinced that they are the center of the universe. Everyone views the world in relation to how what happens in it affects, or relates to, them. I remember a creative writing course I took in the early nineties. I wanted to learn more about writing fiction well, and I thought an adult class might be useful. It was. I learned something about writing the first night. The professor's first words were, "Good writing has resonance." As a musician, I immediately understood what the teacher meant. Writing has to be something the reader feels, or makes an intellectual connection with. When you listen, think of it as reading the story of the speaker's life and mind.

"I have never learned a single thing in this life while I was talking." I committed that statement to memory a long time ago as a way to remind myself to stop talking and listen. From my point of view, if more people heard and followed that little piece of advice, there would be a lot less trouble in the world. Listening requires restraint, yes. But when you really listen, you demonstrate interest. You show respect. How can that formula fail to help you to sell (or connect, or communicate, or parent, or date, or lead) without being a jerk?

Engage

Listening is required before you can actively engage others. In order to sell without being a jerk, you must engage your suspects, prospects, and clients. This means that your responses (listen 80 percent/respond 20 percent) must consistently be based on what they have just said. Many times during my sales career I have witnessed salespeople ignore what a prospect has just told them and go on to deliver a feature/benefit statement or start to talk about price or delivery. If the prospect is talking about how he or she uses a particular item or service, but does not mention that he or she wants to buy, I have to be careful about what I say next, because in natural, unfettered conversation, there should be a rhythm and natural flow. When a prospect says, "We usually don't look at new vendors at this time of year," the salesperson who responds with, "Well, we could offer you 30-day terms," is obviously not listening. If you do not listen to your prospects, they will be less likely to engage. If they are not engaged, you can call your exchange with them anything you like, but you can't call it a "great conversation" or a "good call."

Moving Conversations Forward is fully dependent on you engaging the other person. This cannot happen unless you are enthusiastic and disciplined, and *demonstrate* that discipline by listening to what your prospects have to say. Your ability to focus will be tested by whether or not you have your prospects engaged, or they are staring out the window or at their email screen while you are busy babbling on about your product's or service's great features and benefits.

Ask

To engage your suspects, prospects, customers, employees —and everyone else in your life—requires only that you follow this simple, three-step path:

1. Ask

2. Listen

3. Repeat

Don't sell like a jerk. Be patient. Be productive. Be a good seller. The list above (ask, listen, repeat) looks suspiciously like LATHER, RINSE, REPEAT, doesn't it? Whoever thought of putting those instructions on a bottle of shampoo must have gotten a huge bonus, because what that simple instruction resulted in was a doubling of sales of that shampoo. Think about it. Isn't that *awesome?!* If the world was used to putting shampoo in their hair, lathering, rinsing and then stopping there, think about how much more they sold when people adopted the new instructions!

The questions you can ask are endless, yet the only question that really resonates, and will enable you to engage the person you are in conversation with is the next one out of your mouth. I recommend you make it a Million-Dollar Question. Ask people what they want, think, hope for, or enjoy. They will tell you. All you need to do is ask, listen, repeat.

Honesty

Jokes about honesty—more to the point, the lack of it—in the selling profession are countless. I will quote a famous adage about honesty, and add a bit of a wisecrack, to make my point: "Honesty is the best policy, because when you are honest, you never have to remember what you said to anyone." It's funny, but it is also true. Simply put, you will never go wrong if you are honest with people. In the selling life, being honest may not get you *this* transaction, but it very well may get you several transactions in the future with the same prospect.

I have had people "go away" before I closed them because my fees were too high. This is tough to take, but pricing can very often be a qualifier! One recent prospect responded to my fee quote with, "That's a lot of money." My response, "You are absolutely right. What do you want to do next?" (He ended up hiring me to speak at his national meeting.) My point: I am up front, I do not waiver, and I am honest with my prospects. If what I offer does not fit financially, philosophically, or at any other level, I am the first one to point it out.

Remember, the appropriate time to celebrate the sale is after the commission check clears your bank. Until you have a signed deal, you don't have *any* deal. The flip side of this is, you can only lose what you already have. If I don't have the deal, and the prospect walks away, nothing in my life has changed. I would rather be honest and have the prospect convince me that we should do business together, because when I say something, he or she hears an opinion, but when the prospect says it, it's a fact.

Now, go and do likewise. Just sell! I repeat my definition of selling: "To have people feel good about making a positive decision to move the conversation forward with me, today." As I said early in the book, I have worked on iterations of that definition for several years, before I finally and firmly landed on this one, which I have been satisfied with for the better part of 10 years. Things change—music, technology, quality of service at your favorite restaurant. But not many things about human nature have changed during my selling career. Here are some things that have not changed, and I doubt they ever will:

- People want to be listened to and heard.
- People want to feel important.
- People want to make good decisions.
- People do not want to buy from someone they feel is a jerk.

Regardless of your intentions, if someone feels or thinks you are a jerk, they will not concern themselves with whether or not you are putting on an act. "Hard closers" who say "But I don't act like that with my friends and family" are missing the point. There should not be any reason for you to sell like a jerk. Just sell! You will not sell to everyone, and no matter how much you think a person or company should buy from you, it has to be a good idea to *them*. That statement must come from their mouth, not yours. Moving Conversations Forward in incremental steps (sometimes large, quantum-level, sometimes small, measured steps) is all you can hope for. If you generate the activity required to put yourself and your offer in front of enough people, the law of averages will take effect. If you touch enough people, one of them will buy.

I, of course, hope, wish, and pray that as a result of reading this little book you will approach your prospects as worthy and respected potential relationships. Sell. Move the Conversation Forward. Get invited back, instead of asking for permission and hoping for the best. You have ultimate control of something that affects every selling day: how you act and react.

Close

In sales environments all across this country, salespeople talk about, joke about, and *avoid* closing every day. Several books have been written to address this very issue.

Allow me to offer you the best insight and advice I can about closing:

- You must close early and often.
- "Closing" is not the same as "closure."
- Closing is defined as *coming to agreement.*

Note the third point: It does not say that closing is about getting the deal. It is about taking everything we have discussed and putting it all into disciplined, enthusiastic, focused, honest, practice. Closing is not a dirty word; wanting to close someone is not tantamount to mind control. Closing simply means *coming to agreement.* Closing occurs when I ask the Million-Dollar Question, "What would you like to see happen next?" and the prospect:

- Asks for an order form, or
- Asks me to confirm an available date on my calendar, or
- Asks me how long it will take to begin the installation.

When one of these questions comes out of the prospect's mouth, it is a fact, it is a great idea, and it is a confirmed close.

I do not attempt to close the prospect by offering multiple options, and then go silent, waiting for him or her to say something like, "I want to buy from you now." People in the business world rarely speak that way. You will hear things like, "We are excited about getting going with you." "We look forward to working with you." Or, "It will be great to bring our two groups together."

Sell, and sell a lot. Sell, and sell often. Sell as if your life depended upon it. Because *it does*!

LOVE IT OR LEAVE IT

This book is a collection of my ideas, thoughts, and opinions. My overarching and nonnegotiable opinion is that if you do not love selling, you should find another profession as quickly as you can afford to.

Selling for a living does not automatically make you a jerk. Selling like a jerk because you think it will increase your income *does* make you a jerk. This selling life is not for everyone. It is for the select few—the people who are tough-minded and kind-hearted. It is for people who respond to a day or two of frustration by becoming motivated to improve what they are doing, instead of looking for someone or something to blame. Selling is for people with a sense of humor and respect for humanity, who are willing to make regular, disciplined investments in their own financial future.

I love this profession, and I hope you love it, as well. If you love it, encourage other great people to join us. Learn to be great at it. Be proud of it.

I will close this chapter, and this book, with a short list of simple requests.

- If the book does not resonate with you, pass it on to someone else who sells, and see if it works for him or her.

- If you put my suggestions into practice and find that they do not work, contact me.

- If at this stage, you are still unsure whether you can sell without being a jerk, do everyone a favor: *Don't sell anymore.* (Believe me, I recognize how people may react to this statement.)

I hope this book sets your selling life off on a new path of fun, revenue, and selling without being a jerk. Ultimately, I hope it prompts you to reach out to my company, to tell your success story. I would also love to hear your painfully true selling story. Send them to: coachk@generatorinc.com.

Now please, go sell without being a jerk!

Index

About the Author

J ohn Klymshyn is *not* a jerk! At least that's what his family and friends will tell you. He *is*, however, the global authority on selling to human beings. His humor, techniques, and from-the-trenches wisdom have won him international acclaim as an author, coach, speaker, and executive confidant. His marquee client list directly reflects his belief that sales is an honorable profession, and that the profession can be practiced and mastered through skill, patience, and humor.

How to Sell without Being a JERK! is Klymshyn's third book, following *Move the Sale Forward* (Silver Lake, 2004), and *The Ultimate Sales Managers' Guide* (John Wiley & Sons, Inc., 2006), the latter an international success. He is also the author of more than 125 articles on sales, communication, human connections, parenting, making money, laughing at yourself, and getting along with others.

Klymshyn is a sales and sales management veteran of over 24 years, having built, fixed, or vigorously motivated sales teams in the staffing, cellular, advertising, and high-tech industries. One former employee and current company owner has said of Klymshyn's approach, "If you listen to John, you will make a lot of money, and have a lot of fun doing it!"

Currently, Klymshyn is the president of The Business Generator, Inc., a sales, sales management, and branding consulting firm based in Valencia, California. He speaks at conventions and meetings throughout the year for organizations looking to increase sales and balance the lives of their performers.

Klymshyn lives his dream of contributing to other people's lives through teaching, coaching, writing, and laughing loudly at every opportunity. John and Terri, his wife of 23 years, proudly boast of their two children: Lauren, their daughter, is a college student; and John III, their oldest, is a digital film editor currently working in television.

Klymshyn has been writing fiction and nonfiction for over 30 years.